Michael M. Dediu

Da Vinci, Michelangelo, Rembrandt, Rodin

A chronological and photographic documentary

DERC Publishing House
Tewksbury (Boston), Massachusetts, U. S. A.

Copyright ©2018 by Michael M. Dediu

All rights reserved

Published and printed in the
United States of America
On the Great Seal of the United States are included:
E Pluribus Unum (Out of many, one)
Annuit Coeptis (He has approved of the undertakings)
Novus Ordo Seclorum (New order of the ages)

Library of Congress Control Number: 2018912678

Dediu, Michael M.

Da Vinci, Michelangelo, Rembrandt, Rodin
A chronological and photographic documentary

ISBN-13: 978-1-93975777-7

Preface

These great artists have very good aphorisms.

Leonardo da Vinci: "It had long since come to my attention that people of accomplishment rarely sat back and let things happen to them. They went out and happened to things." "The natural desire of good men is knowledge." "Learning never exhausts the mind."

Michelangelo: "I saw the angel in the marble and carved until I set him free." Every block of stone has a statue inside it, and it is the task of the sculptor to discover it." "The greater danger for most of us lies not in setting our aim too high and falling short; but in setting our aim too low, and achieving our mark." "Painting is a music and a melody to be understood only by the intellect, and that with difficulty."

Rembrandt: "Painting is the grandchild of nature." "Without atmosphere a painting is nothing".

Rodin: "Patience is also a form of action." "Nothing is a waste of time, if you use the experience wisely."

This book is focused on these artists, offering, in a chronological order (this chronological order gives the correct perspective of events and personalities at any given time, because the time determines everything), a variety of relevant information not only about them, but also about the numerous other personalities and important events, which took place during their remarkable working years. There are also many attractive and historic photographs, some of reproductions which we accumulated over the years – I want to thank my wife for her assistance. I want also to mention reports which show that Jeff Bezos works hard to improve Amazon's performance for its customers, and for its employees.

This book brings a rainbow of practical information, and this will certainly enhance everybody's joie de vivre.

Michael M. Dediu, Ph. D.

Tewksbury (Boston), U. S. A., 7 November 2018

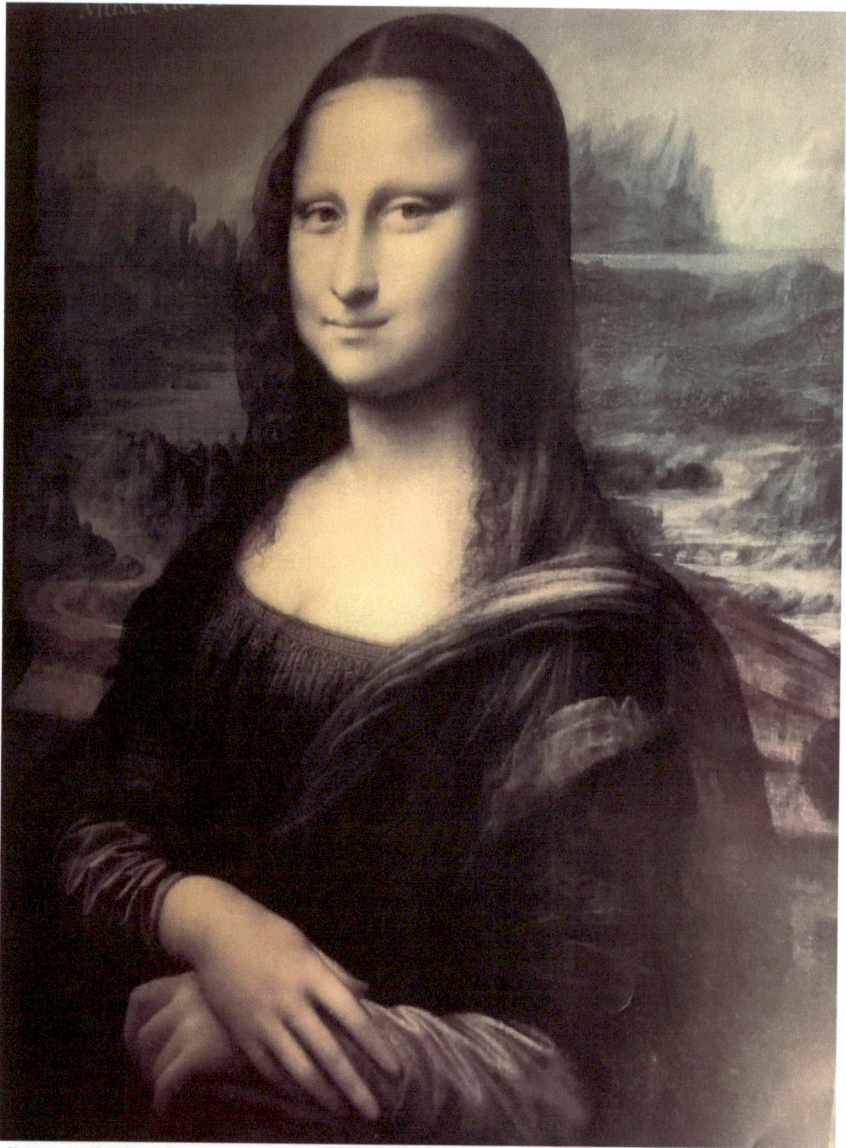

Copy of Mona Lisa (or La Gioconda, detail), 1506, by Leonardo da Vinci

Table of Contents

Preface 3

Table of Contents 5

Chapter 1. Leonardo da Vinci 7

Chapter 2. Michelangelo 11

Chapter 3. Rembrandt 85

Chapter 3. Auguste Rodin 116

Bibliography 148

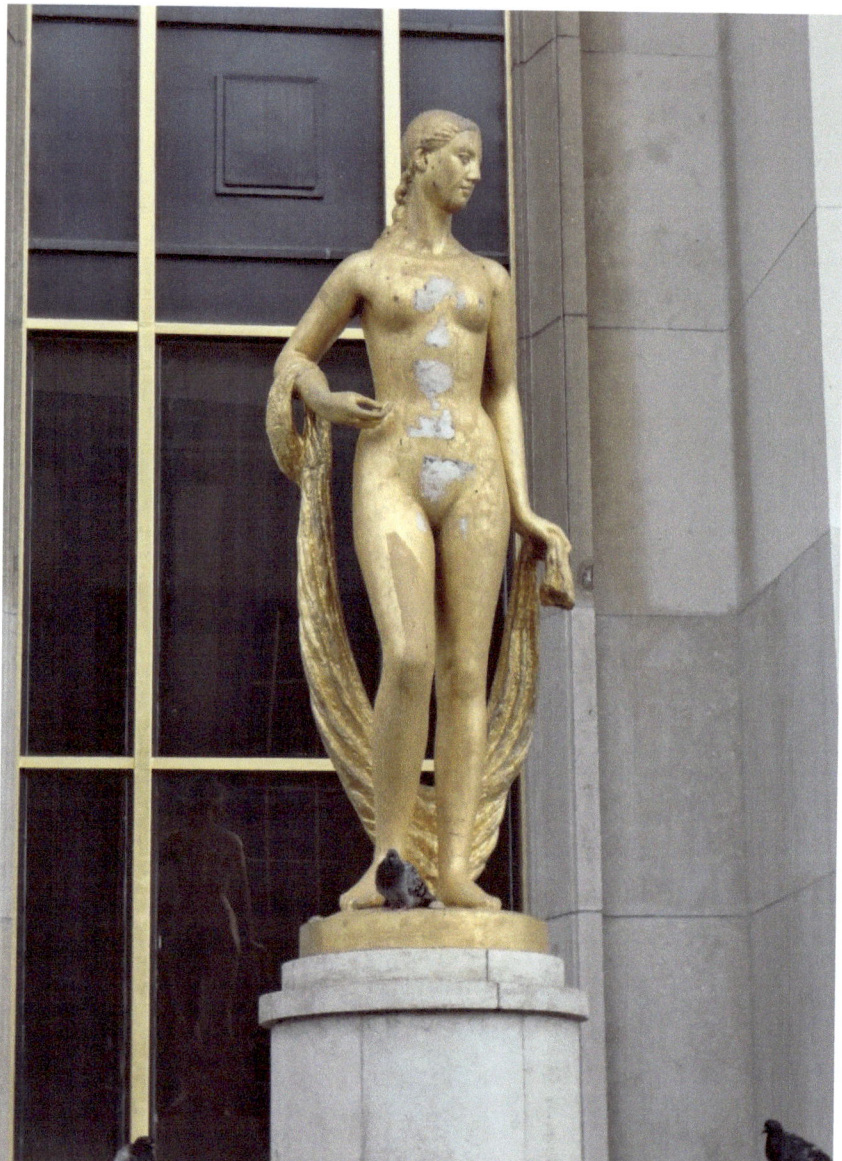

Paris: The statue "Flore" (1937) by Marcel Gimond (1894 – 1961, French sculptor, studied at the Beaux-Arts Academy in Lyon, and then he was the student in turn of both Aristide Maillol (1861 – 1944) and Auguste Rodin (1840 – 1917)), on the south-west façade of Palais de Chaillot (1937, named after a former village which was here, with architectural, naval and ethnographic museums), on the hill of the Trocadéro.

Chapter 1. Leonardo da Vinci

1452 – 15 April – Birth of Leonardo da Vinci (full name Leonardo di ser Piero da Vinci, 15 April 1452, Anchiano near Vinci (25 km west of Florence, on a Tuscan hill, in the lower valley of the Arno River), Republic of Florence (ruled by Medici) – 2 May 1519, Amboise, Kingdom of France, aged 67 years and 17 days), Italian polymath whose areas of interest included invention, painting, sculpting, architecture, science, music, mathematics, engineering, literature, anatomy, geology, astronomy, optics, botany, hydrodynamics, writing, history, and cartography, but he did not publish his findings. He is the father of paleontology, ichnology, and architecture, and is one of the greatest painters of all time.

His father was a middle-class wealthy Messer (old Italian for Signore (gentleman)) and notary in Firenze, Piero da Vinci, 25, (1427 - 9 July 1504, aged 77), and his mother a peasant woman, Caterina di Meo Lippi (probably 20 years old). Leonardo's full birth name was "Leonardo di ser Piero da Vinci", meaning "Leonardo, (son) of (Mes)ser Piero from Vinci". The inclusion of the title "ser" indicated that Leonardo's father was a gentleman. The father married Albiera Amadori, 16, (1436 – 1465, aged 29), but no children.

27 July – Birth of Ludovico Sforza (27 July 1452 – 27 May 1508, aged 55.8, Regent of Milan 7 Oct 1480 – 21 Oct 1494, Duke of Milan 21 Oct 1494 – 6 Sep 1499).

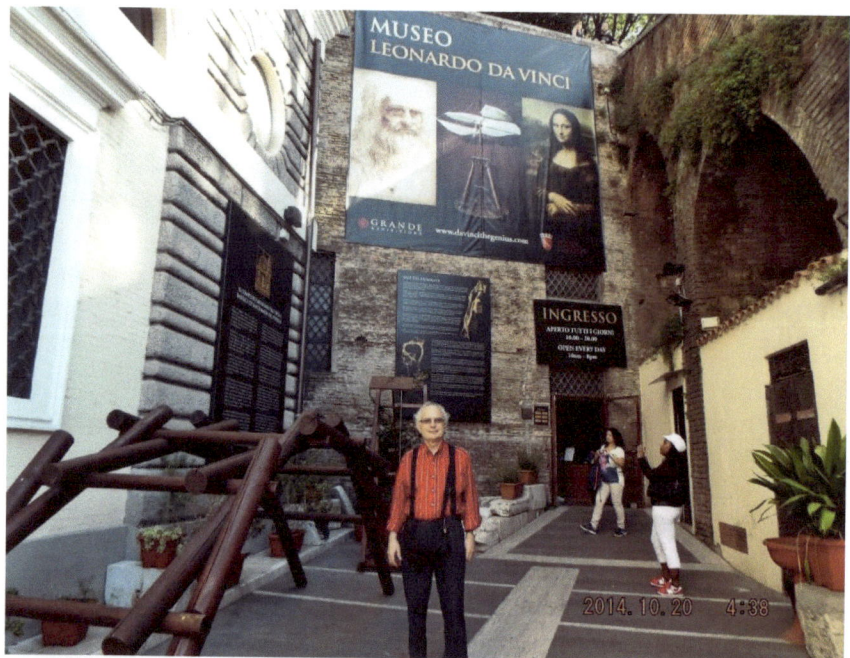

Italy, Rome, Piazza del Popolo, south of Basilica Santa Maria del Popolo, Museo Leonardo da Vinci (1452 – 1519, mathematician, painter, sculptor, architect, musician, inventor, writer, anatomist).

1455 – Leonardo was 3 years old, with his mother, when his half-sister Piera di Meo Lippi was born by his mother, 23, and married to Acattabriga di Piero di Luca.

18 February – Death of Beato Angelico (Fra Angelico, born Guido di Pietro; c. 1395 – February 18, 1455, aged c. 59.5), Italian painter, with his famous painting "Annunciation" (c. 1430, when he was 35) in Diocesan Museum in Cortona.

1 December – Death of Lorenzo Ghiberti (1378 – 1 December 1455, aged 77), born Lorenzo di Bartolo, a Florentine Italian artist best known as the creator, after 50 years of work, of the bronze doors of the Florence Baptistery, later called by Michelangelo the Gates of Paradise. Trained as a goldsmith and sculptor, he established an important workshop for sculpture in metal. His book of Commentarii contains important writing on art, as well as what may be the earliest surviving autobiography by any artist.

1457 – Leonardo, 5, who was until now with his mother Caterina (circa 25) in Anchiano, was taken by his father Piero, 30, and lived in the household of his father, grandparents and uncle in the small town of Vinci.

1458 – Leonardo was 6, with his father Piero, 31, in Vinci, when his half-sister Maria di Meo Lippi was born by his mother, 26, in Anchiano.

1459 – Leonardo was 7 when his father began to provide him with some informal education in Latin and mathematics, especially geometry.
Birth of Lorenzo di Credi (1459 – 12 Jan 1537, aged 78), Italian painter.

1463 – 24 February - Leonardo was 10.9 when Giovanni Pico della Mirandola was born (24 February 1463 – 17 November 1494, aged 31.7), Italian nobleman and philosopher.

1465 – Leonardo was 13 when his step-mother Albiera Amadori, who took good care of him for 8 years, and noticed his talent for painting, died at only 29.

1466 – Leonardo was 14 when his father, 39, appreciating Leonardo's talent for painting, apprenticed him, for 10 years, to the artist Andrea di Cione, known as Verrocchio, 31, (1435 – 1488, aged 53). He also received training in the anatomy of the human body. Verrocchio's bottega (workshop) was well known in Florence. He apprenticed as a garzone (studio boy) to Andrea del Verrocchio, the leading Florentine painter and sculptor of his day (for 7 more years, after which his pupil Leonardo becomes the best). Other famous painters apprenticed or associated with the workshop include:
- Domenico Ghirlandaio (2 June 1448 – 11 Jan 1494, aged 45.6), 3.8 years older than Leonardo;
- Pietro Perugino (1446 – 1523, aged 77), 6 years older than Leonardo, but died 4 years after him.
- Sandro Botticelli (1445 – 17 May 1510, aged 65), 7 years older than Leonardo, and

- Lorenzo di Credi (1459 – 12 Jan 1537, aged 78), 7 years younger than Leonardo.

Leonardo, for 10 years, had both theoretical training and a vast range of technical skills, including drafting, chemistry, metallurgy, metal working, plaster casting, leather working, mechanics and carpentry as well as the artistic skills of drawing, painting, sculpting and modelling. Leonardo collaborated with Verrocchio on some paintings.

13 December – Death of Donatello at 80 (1386 – 13 Dec 1466, great Italian sculptor, teacher of Verrocchio).

1468 – Leonardo was 16 when his father Piero, 41, married for the second time to Francesca Lanfredini, 22, (1446 – 1474, aged 28), who also died without children.

1469 – 3 May – Birth of Niccolò di Bernardo dei Machiavelli (3 May 1469 – 21 June 1527, aged 58.1), Italian diplomat, politician, historian, philosopher, humanist, writer, playwright and poet.

2 December - Leonardo was 17.6 when Lorenzo de' Medici, 20.9, became Lord of Florence.

1472 – Leonardo, 20, started the first small (59 cm by 14 cm) painting "The Annunciation", with Andrea del Verrocchio – finished in less than 3 years, by 1475.
Leonardo qualified as a master in the Guild of Saint Luke, the guild of artists and doctors of medicine.

His father, 45, set him up in his own workshop, however Leonardo continued to collaborate with Verrocchio.

1473 – 5 August - Leonardo, 21.3, had his earliest known dated work - a drawing in pen and ink of the Arno Valley, Landscape of the Arno Valley, now at Uffizi in Florence.

Chapter 2. Michelangelo

<u>**1475**</u> – 6 March – Leonardo was 22 years 10 months and 19 days when Michelangelo di Lodovico Buonarroti Simoni or Michelangelo was born (6 March 1475, Caprese (20 km northeast of Arezzo, 40 km north of Cortona, 60 km southeast of Florence) – 18 February 1564, aged 88.9 (just 16 days before 89)), great Italian sculptor, painter, and architect. His father Ludovico di Leonardo di Buonarroti Simoni, 30.7, (11 June 1444 – 1534, aged 90, had 6 brothers and sisters), was a small banker in Florence, but the bank failed, and he briefly took a government post in Caprese, where Michelangelo was born. At the time of Michelangelo's birth, his father was the town's Judicial administrator, and podestà or local administrator of Chiusi della Verna. Michelangelo's mother was Francesca di Neri del Miniato di Siena, 25, (c. 1450 – 1881, aged 31). Several months after Michelangelo's birth, the family returned to Florence, where he was raised. Michelangelo had an older brother – Leonardo Buonarroti Simoni, 2 years old, born on 16 Nov 1473.

10 December – Death of Paolo Uccello (1397 – 10 December 1475, aged 78), born Paolo di Dono, Italian painter and mathematician, who is remembered for his pioneering work on visual perspective in art.

Leonardo, 23, started the second larger (2.17 m long) painting "The Annunciation", alone – finished in less than 5 years, by 1480 – this is his first complete painting. The same subject was painted before by Fra Angelico, and about the same time by Signorelli.

Leonardo was 23 when his father Piero, 48, married his third wife Margherita di Guglielmo, 17, (1458 – 1487, aged 29, who gave birth in 12 years to six children: Antonio (1476), Maddalena (1477), Giulian (1479), Lorenzo (1484), Violante (1485) and Domenico (1486)).

<u>**1476**</u> – Leonardo, 24, painted the portrait of Ginevra de'Benci, 19, from the aristocratic class of Firenze (Florence).

He left the Verrocchio's workshop.

Birth of his half-brother Antonio da Vinci, when his father was 49.

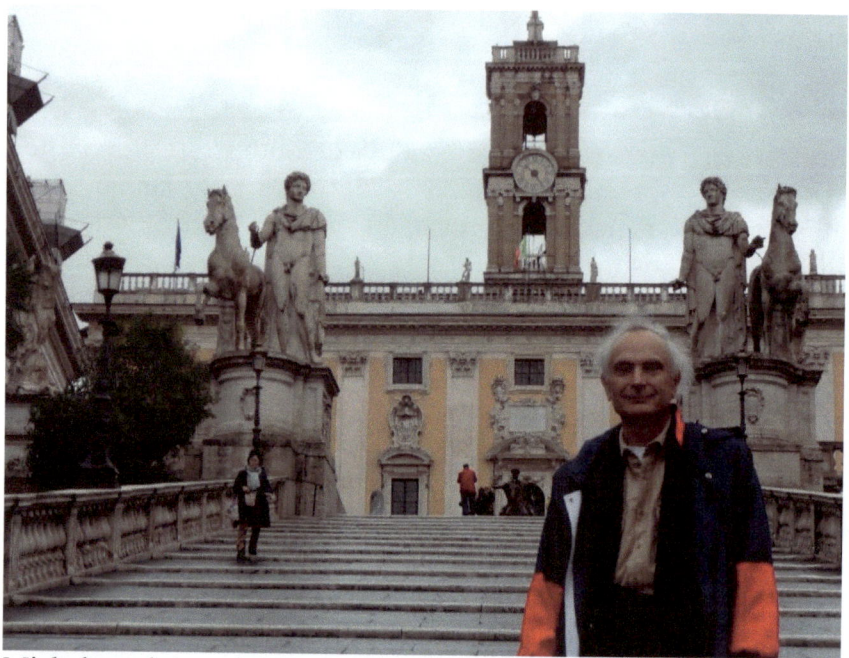

Michelangelo's stair (the cordonata) to Piazza del Campidoglio. The statues of Castor and Pollux and Palazzo Senatorio (back).

1477 – Leonardo was 25 when his half-sister Maddalena da Vinci was born, his father being 50.

26 May - Michelangelo was 2.1 years old when his second brother Buonarroto Buonarroti Simoni was born (26 May 1477 – 2 July 1528, aged 51.1).

1478 – January - Leonardo received an independent commission to paint an altarpiece for the Chapel of St. Bernard in the Palazzo Vecchio, but it was not completed.

Leonardo, 26, painted Madonna and Child with Flowers (also known as the Benois Madonna).

He also started the oil painting the Madonna of the Carnation (or Madonna with vase, or Madonna with child), and his sketches of the self-propelled cart (folio 812r of the Codex Atlanticus) – both finished in less than 2 years, by 1480.

Leonardo left Verrocchio's studio, and was no longer a resident at his father's house.

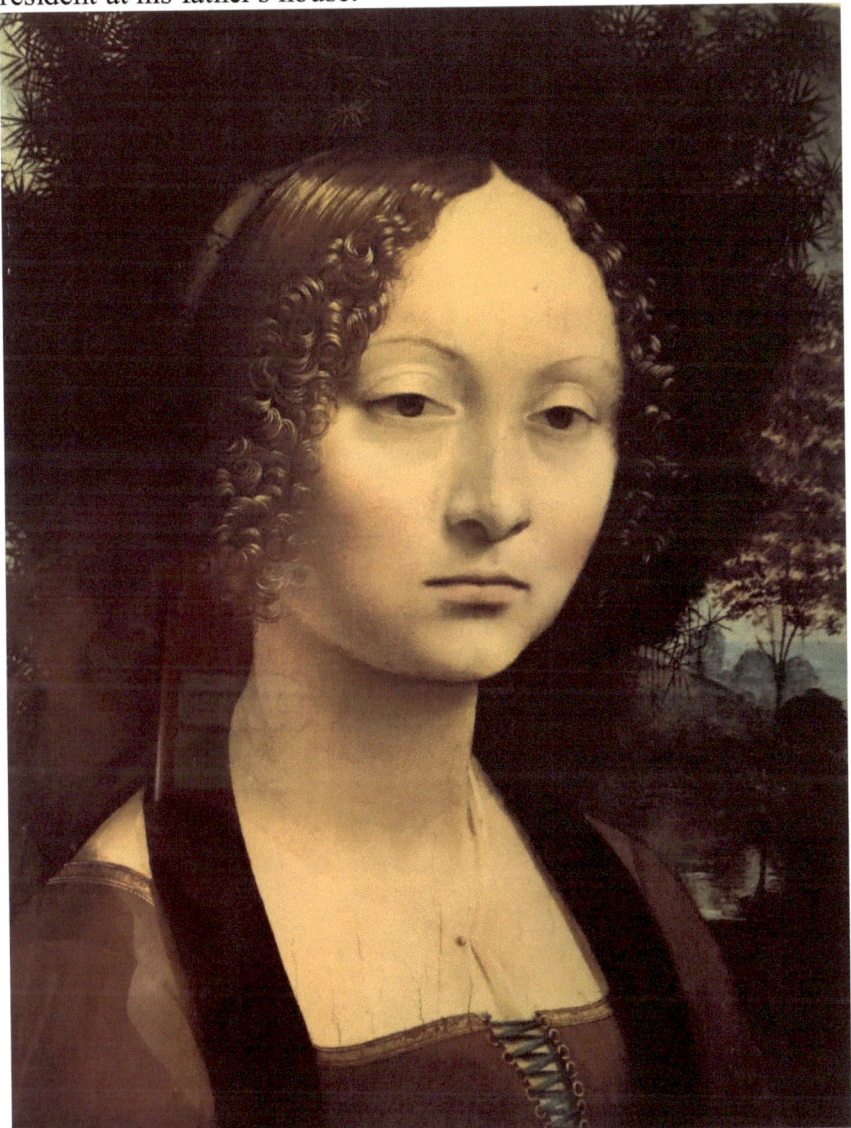

Leonardo da Vinci, 26, 1478, Wreath of Laurel, Palm, and Juniper with a Scroll inscribed (portrait of Ginevra de'Benci, 21, from the aristocratic class of Firenze (Florence), oil on wood, acquired by the National Gallery of Art in Washington, D.C. in 1967).

1479 – Leonardo was 27 when his half-brother Giulian da Vinci was born, his father being 52.

Perugino, 33, was the first to start painting the walls of the Sistine Chapel. Then other painters from Florence were called to the Vatican, including Domenico Ghirlandaio, 31, a master in fresco painting, perspective, figure drawing and portraiture, who had the largest workshop in Florence.

11 March - Michelangelo was 4 years old when his third brother Giovan Simone Buonarroti Simoni was born (11 March 1479 – 9 Jan 1548, aged 68.8).

1480 – Leonardo, 28, painted Saint Jerome in Wilderness (during his retreat to the Syrian desert), but unfinished.

7 October - Ludovico Sforza, 28.3, became Regent of Milan for 14 years.

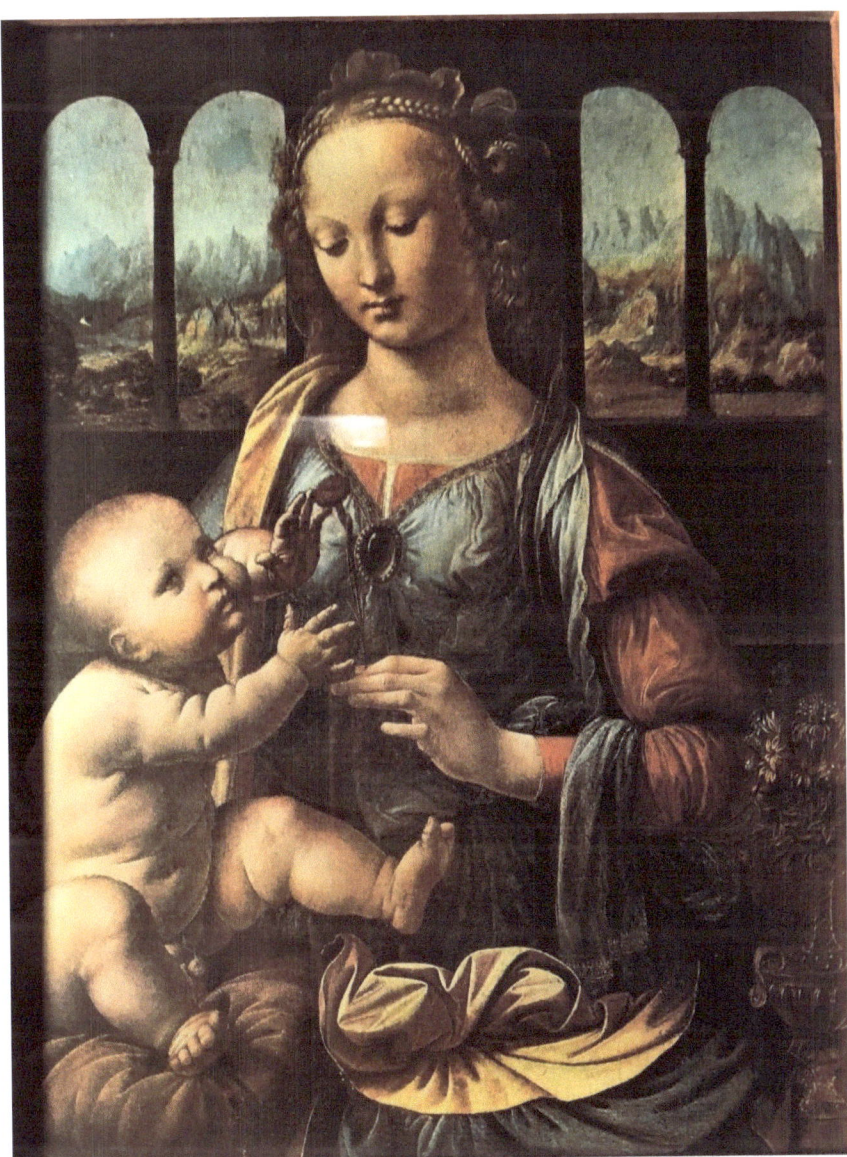

Leonardo da Vinci, 28, 1480, Madonna of the Carnation

1481 – March - Leonardo, 29, started painting "The Adoration of the Magi" (2.5 m by 2.5 m) based on the commission given to him by the Augustinian monks of San Donato a Scoperto in Florence, but it was not completed, because he was sent to Milano in 1482.

22 January - Michelangelo was 5.9 years old when his fourth brother Sigismondo Buonarroti Simoni was born (22 Jan 1481 – 13 Nov 1555, aged 74.8).

Then his mother passed away. During his mother's earlier prolonged illness, and after her death, Michelangelo lived with a nanny and her husband, a stonecutter, in the town of Settignano (6 km northeast of Florence), where his father owned a marble quarry and a small farm. There he gained his love for marble.

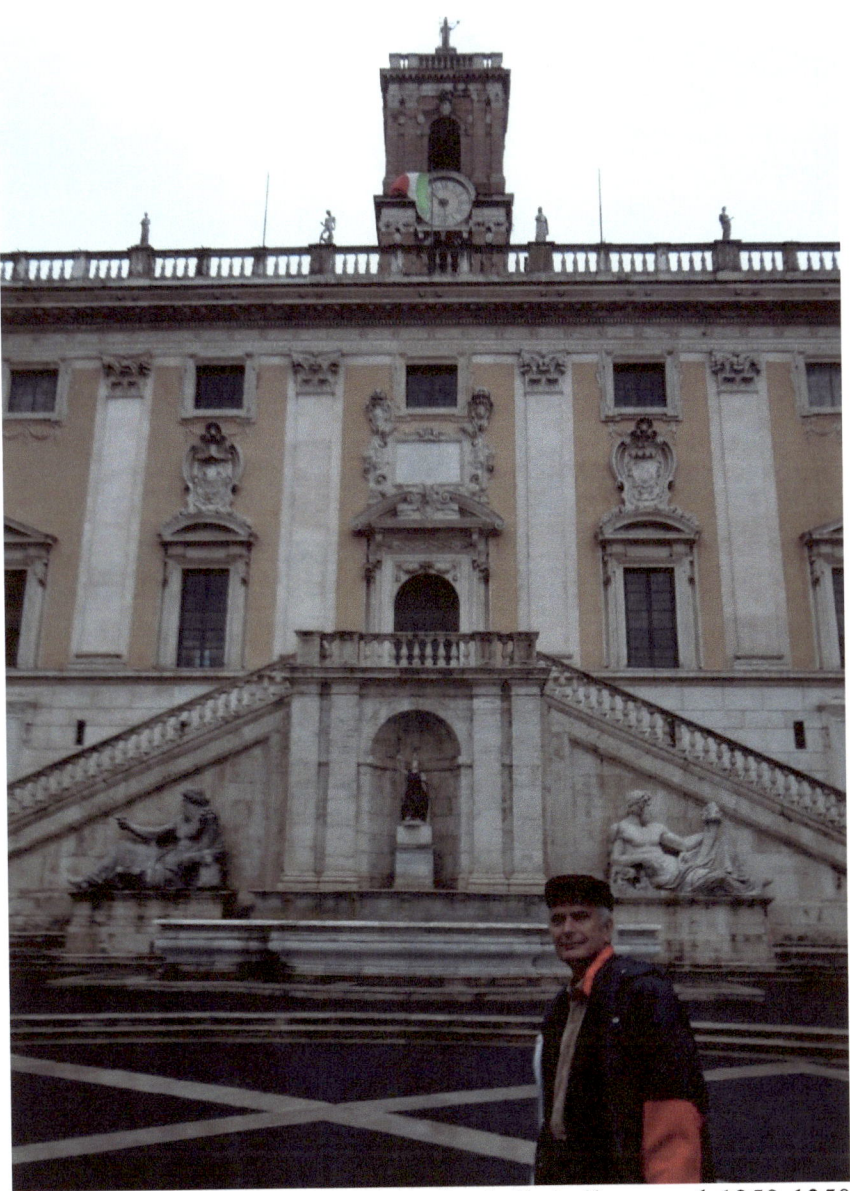

Palazzo Senatorio, now Rome's city hall, built around 1250-1350 atop the Tabularium (78 BC, housed the archives of the ancient Rome), re-used blocks from the Tabularium in the left side of the Palazzo and in a corner of the bell tower. It was modified by Michelangelo around 1535, with its double ramp of stairs being designed by him. The fountain in front of the staircase features the river gods of the Tiber and the Nile, and Dea Roma (Minerva).

1482 – Leonardo, 30, being also a musician, created a silver lyre in the shape of a horse's head. Lorenzo de' Medici (il Magnifico), 33, (1 January 1449 – 8 April 1492, aged 43.3, Lord of Florence from the age of 20.9, for 22.4 years (2 Dec 1469 – 8 April 1492)) sent Leonardo to Milan, bearing the lyre as a gift, to secure peace with Ludovico Sforza (il Moro), 30, (27 July 1452 – 27 May 1508, aged 55.8, Regent of Milan 7 Oct 1480 – 21 Oct 1494, Duke of Milan 21 Oct 1494 – 6 Sep 1499). At this time, Leonardo wrote a letter describing the many and diverse things that he could achieve in the field of engineering, and informing Ludovico that he could also paint. Based on this letter, Leonardo worked in Milano from this year, for 17 years, until 1499.

1483 – Leonardo, 31, was commissioned to paint the first Madonna of the Rocks (or the Virgin of the Rocks, 2 m by 1.2 m) for the Confraternity of the Immaculate Conception – this is the first of the two different paintings, which are almost identical – finished in less than 3 years, by 1486, and remained at the chapel of the Confraternity. He will start the second 12 years later, in 1495.

He also started his sketches of the design for a parachute.

1484 – Leonardo was 32 when his half-brother Lorenzo da Vinci was born, his father being 57.

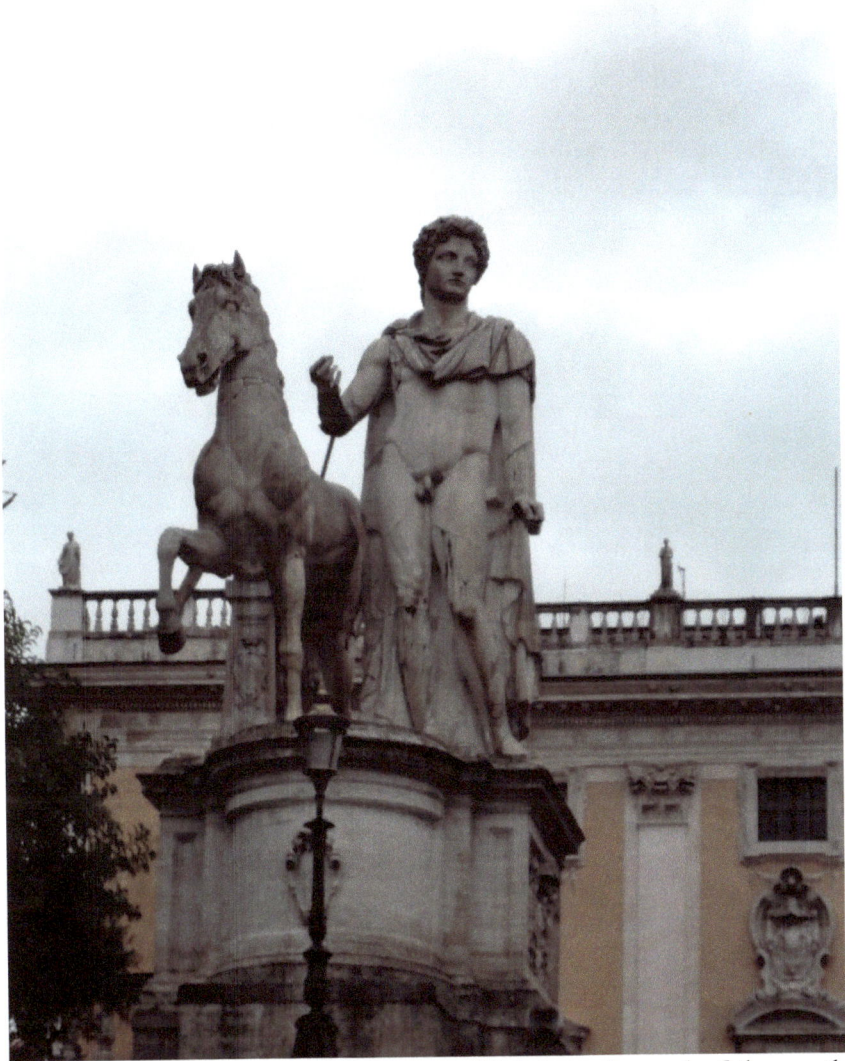

The statue of Castor and his horse, which is at the end of the north railings of Michelangelo's epic and wide-ramped stair (the cordonata), that is gradually ascending the hill to reach the high Piazza del Campidoglio. Palazzo Senatorio (back, now Rome's city hall), built around 1250-1350 atop the Tabularium (78 BC, housed the archives of the ancient Rome), re-used blocks from the Tabularium, and was modified by Michelangelo around 1535.

1485 – Leonardo, 33, started his sketches of the design for a giant crossbow, a scythed chariot, and a tank.

Spring - Leonardo travelled to Hungary on behalf of Ludovico, 33, to meet Matthias Corvinus, 42, (23 Feb 1443, Kolozsvar, Hungary, (now Cluj-Napoca, Romania) – 6 April 1490, aged 47.1, now King of Hungary, Croatia and Bohemia, (latter, 1487 – 1490, he will also be Duke of Austria)) for whom he is believed to have painted a Holy Family.

His half-brother Violante da Vinci was born, his father being 58.

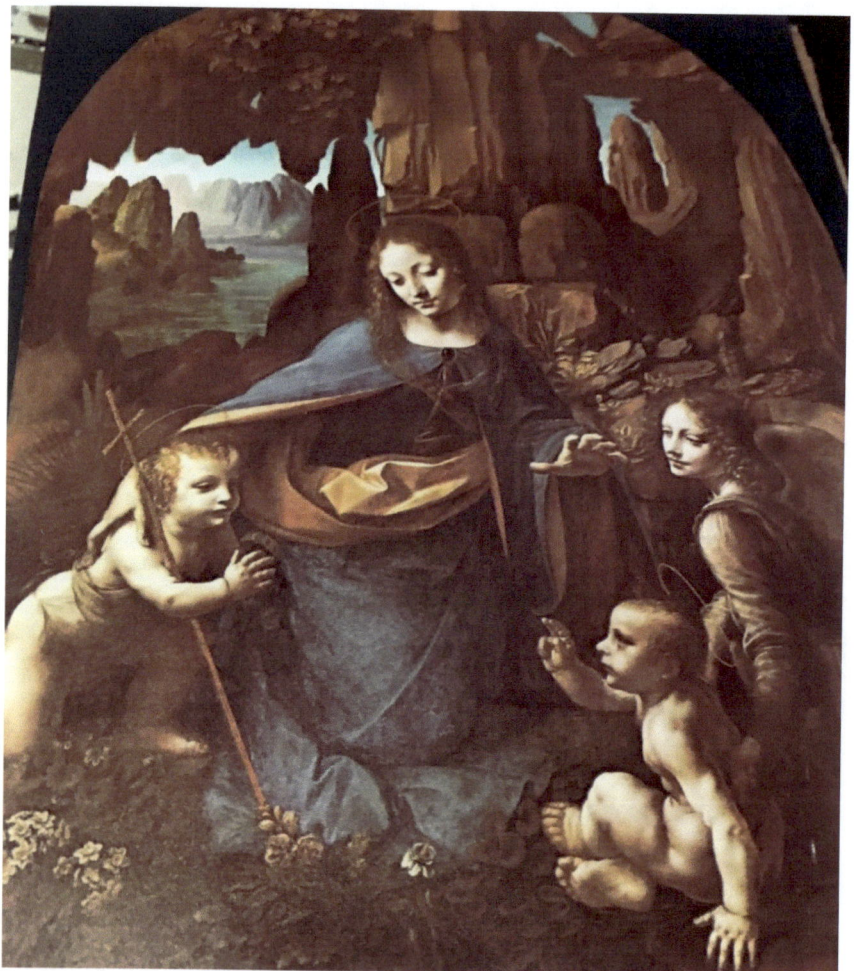

Leonardo da Vinci, 33, 1485, Virgin of the Rocks, 1.99 m by 1.22 m, Louvre, Paris.

Michelangelo was 10 years old when he began to attend school in Florence. He was taught for 3 years by humanist Francesco da Urbino (to 1488). Michelangelo's father, 41, remarried with Lucrezia Ubaldini, 30, (c. 1455 – c. 1520, aged c. 65). Michelangelo was more interested to copy paintings from churches, especially the paintings of Giotto (1267 – 8 Jan 1337, aged 69.5).

1486 – Leonardo was 34 when his half-brother Domenico da Vinci was born, his father being 59.
Botticelli, 41, painted The Birth of Venus.

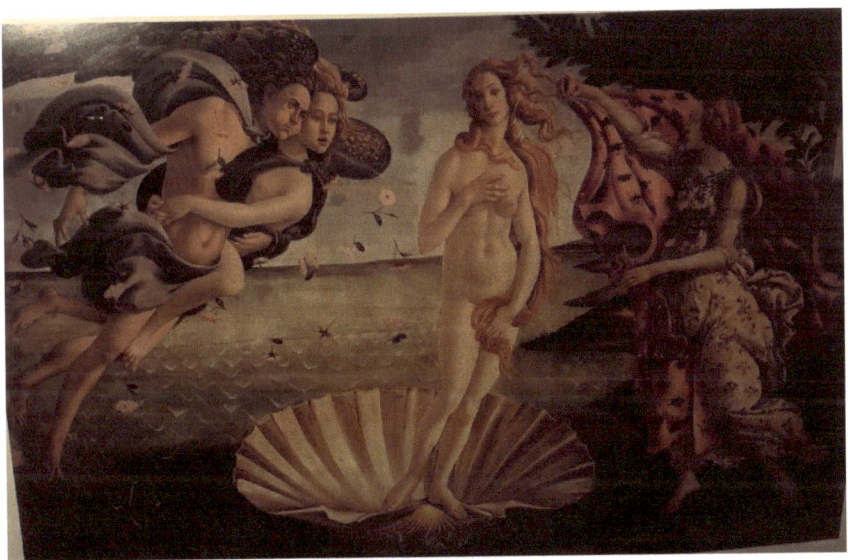

Botticelli, 41, 1486, The Birth of Venus

1487 – Leonardo, 35, draws L'Uomo Vitruviano (the Vitruvian Man, now at Accademia in Venice), which is regarded as a cultural icon, being reproduced on the euro coin, textbooks, etc. Vitruvius was an ancient Roman architect, interested in the proportions of the human body.

He also started his sketches of the design for an armored assault vessel – finished in less than 2 years, by 1489.

1488 – Leonardo, 36, designed his ideal city, he started sketches of the design for a flying machine and for a double-decker bridge – worked on them until 1489 – 1490.

Andrea del Verrocchio died at 53.

The father Piero, 61, married his fourth and final wife, Lucrezia Cortigiani, c. 30, (c. 1458 – c. 1508, aged c. 50, who bore him another six children: Margherita (1491), Benedetto (1492), Pandolfo (1494), Guglielmo (1496), Bartolomeo (1497) and Giovanni (1498)).

Michelangelo was 13 when his father, 44, observing his son's unusual talent, decided to have him as an apprentice to the painter Domenico Ghirlandaio, 40.

1489 – Leonardo, 37, painted Lady with an Ermine, the lady being Cecilia Gallerani – finished by 1490.

Michelangelo was 14 when his father, 45, observing his son's beautiful work, decided to persuade Ghirlandaio, 41, to pay Michelangelo as an artist, which was rare for someone of fourteen.

Lorenzo de' Medici, 40, de facto ruler of Florence, asked Ghirlandaio for his two best pupils, Ghirlandaio sent Michelangelo and Francesco Granacci, 20, (1469 – 30 Nov 1543, aged 74, Italian painter).

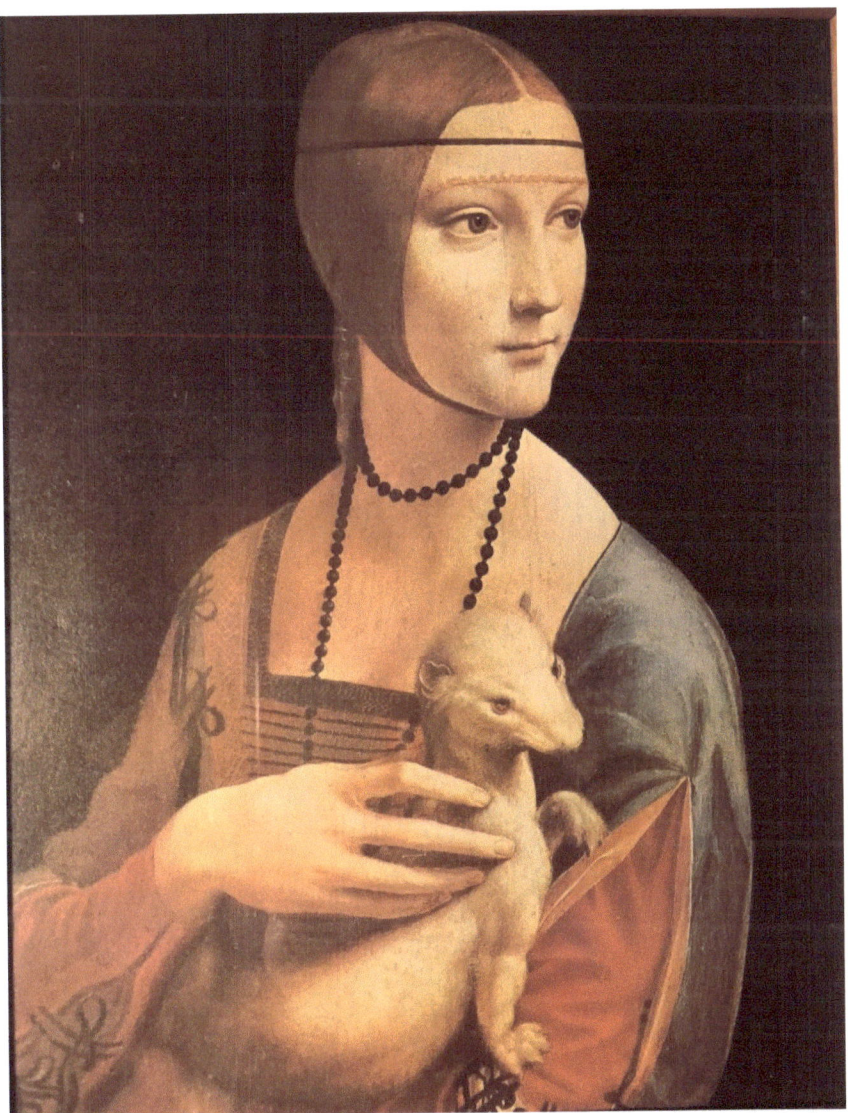

Leonardo da Vinci, 38, 1490, Lady with an Ermine (the lady being Cecilia Gallerani)

1490 – Leonardo, 38, sketches the design for an adding machine – this sketch was discovered on 13 February 1967 in the National Library of Spain, by American scientists.

He also started to write his Codex on the Flight of Birds, which comprises 18 folios, and was finished after 15 years, around 1505.

Leonardo takes as his pupil the 10 years old Gian Giacomo Caprotti da Oreno, better known as Salaì (1480 – 19 Jan 1524, aged 44), Italian artist and pupil of Leonardo da Vinci for 28 years, from 1490 (age 10) to 1518 (age 38); he painted under the name Andrea Salai).

Leonardo painted La belle ferronnière.

Michelangelo was 15 when he began to work for 2 years, until 1492, in the Medici household. He attended the Humanist Academy the Medici had founded, in Neo-Platonic style, and sculpted, for about 2 years, the reliefs Madonna of the Steps, his earliest known work in marble.

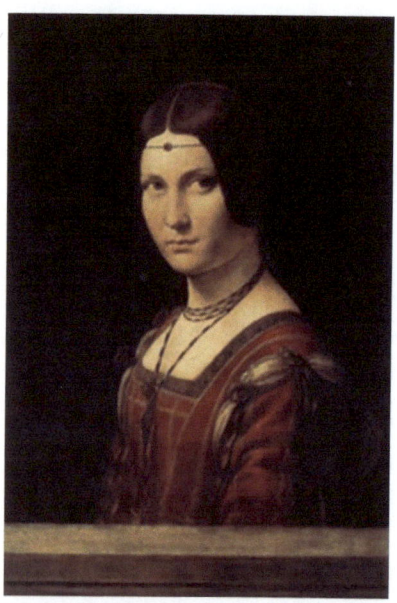

La belle ferronnière, 1490, by Leonardo da Vinci

1491 – Leonardo was 39 when his half-sister Margherita da Vinci was born, his father being 64.

He worked on the designs for a dome for Milan Cathedral (which was started in 1386, and completed in 1965).

Michelangelo, 16, sculpted for 1 year the relief Battle of the Centaurs, based on a theme suggested by Poliziano, 37, (14 July 1454 – 24 Sep 1494, aged 40.2, Italian classical scholar (Homer, Vergilius)), and commissioned by Lorenzo de Medici, 42.

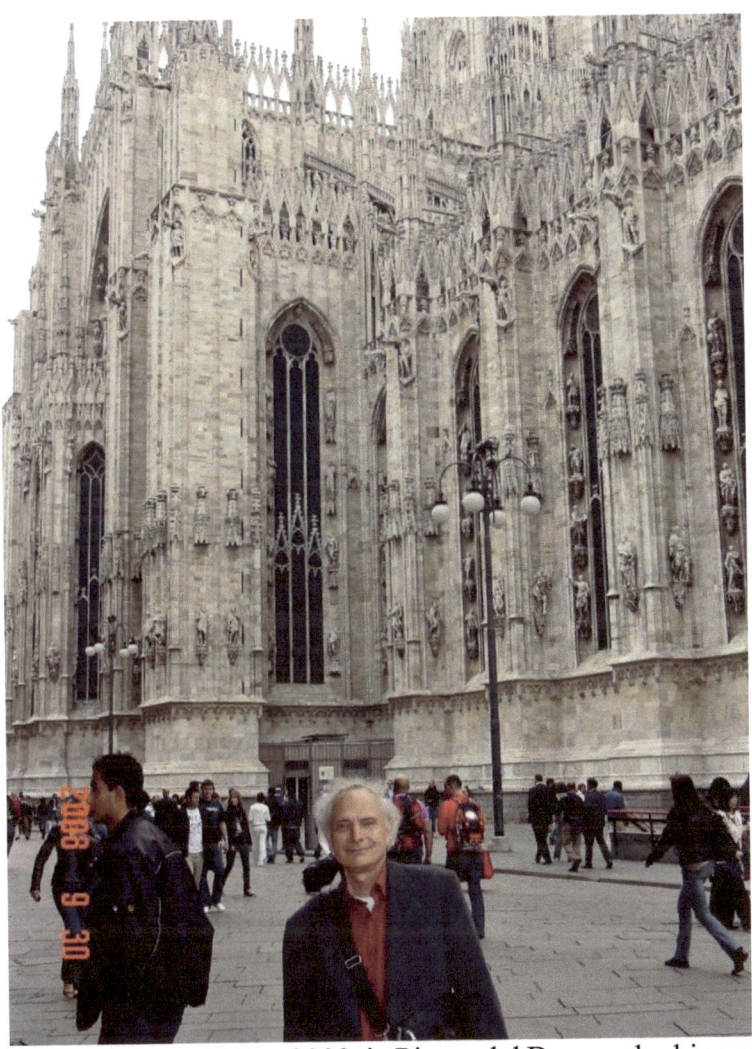

Italia, Milano - 30 Sep 2008, in Piazza del Duomo, looking southeast to the north side of il Duomo (Basilica Cattedrale metropolitana di Santa Maria Nascente, 1386-1965 (579 years), capacity 40,000, length 158.5 m, width 92 m, maximum height 108 m, 135 spires, materials: brick and Candoglia marble, architects: Donato Bramante (1444-1514), Leonardo da Vinci (1452-1519), Giulio Romano (1499-1546), Pellegrino Tibaldi (1527-1596)). On May 20, 1805, Napoleon Bonaparte (1769-1821), about to be crowned King of Italy, ordered the façade to be finished by Pellicani. For this, a statue of Napoleon was placed at the top of one of the spires. Napoleon was crowned King of Italy at the Duomo on May 26, 1805.

1492 – Leonardo, 40, completed the clay model horse for a huge equestrian monument to Francesco Sforza (23 July 1401 – 8 March 1466, aged 64.6), Ludovico's father and predecessor. The clay model surpassed in size the only two large equestrian statues of the Renaissance, Donatello's (1386 – 13 Dec 1466, aged 80, Italian sculptor) "Gattamelata" (1453) in Padua, and Verrocchio's "Bartolomeo Colleoni" (1483-1488) in Venice, and became known as the "Gran Cavallo". Leonardo began making detailed plans for its casting, having 70 tons of bronze set aside.

His half-brother Benedetto da Vinci was born, his father being 65.

Michelangelo, 17, while working with a violent pupil 2.5 years older than him, was struck on the nose by this violent pupil, and this disfigurement is noticeable in all the portraits of Michelangelo.

8 April – Death of Lorenzo de' Medici at 43.3 (1 January 1449 – 8 April 1492, Lord of Florence from the age of 20.9, for 22.4 years (2 Dec 1469 – 8 April 1492)).

After this, Michelangelo returned to his father's house.

12 October – Death of Piero della Francesca (c. 1415 – 12 October 1492, aged 77), Italian painter and mathematician. His painting is characterized by its serene humanism, its use of geometric forms and perspective. His most famous work is the cycle of frescoes The History of the True Cross in the church of San Francesco in the Tuscan town of Arezzo. Piero della Francesca had made a detailed study of perspective, and was the first painter to make a scientific study of light. These studies and Alberti's treatise De Pictura were to have a profound effect on younger artists and in particular on Leonardo's own observations and artworks.

1493 – Leonardo, 41, sketches the design for the Aerial Screw – the first idea of a helicopter.

He begins to financially support his mother Caterina, 61.

Michelangelo, 18, carved a polychrome wooden Crucifix, as a gift to the prior of the Florentine church of Santo Spirito, which had allowed him to do some anatomical studies.

Then he bought a block of marble, and carved a larger than life statue of Hercules, which was sent to France, and subsequently disappeared sometime in the 18th century.

1494 – 11 January – Death of Domenico Ghirlandaio (2 June 1448 – 11 Jan 1494, aged 45.6, Italian painter, 3.8 years older than Leonardo).

Leonardo was 42 when his half-brother Pandolfo da Vinci was born, his father being 67.

20 January - after heavy snowfalls, Lorenzo's heir, Piero de Medici, 21.9, (15 Feb 1472 – 28 Dec 1503, aged 31.8, Reigned for 2 years and 7 months: 9 April 1492 – 9 Nov 1494), commissioned a snow statue, and Michelangelo, 18.7, again entered the court of the Medici.

12 September – Birth of the future King of France Francis I, (12 Sep 1494 – 31 March 1547, aged 52.5, King for 32 years and 3 months: 1 Jan 1515 – 31 March 1547).

21 October - Ludovico Sforza, 42.3, ended to be Regent of Milan (7 Oct 1480 – 21 Oct 1494) and started as Duke of Milan (21 Oct 1494 – 6 Sep 1499).

9 November - the Medici were expelled from Florence as the result of the rise of Fra Girolamo Savonarola, 42.1, (21 Sep 1452 – 23 May 1498, aged 45.6, Ruler for 3.5 years: Nov 1494 – 23 May 1498, Italian Dominican friar and preacher).

Then Michelangelo, 19.6, left the city before the end of the political upheaval, moving to Venice, and then to Bologna. In Bologna, he was commissioned to carve several of the last small figures – including an Angel - for the completion of the Shrine of St. Dominic, in the church dedicated to that saint.

17 November – Death of Giovanni Pico della Mirandola, aged 31.7 (24 February 1463 – 17 November 1494), Italian nobleman and philosopher.

November - Ludovico gave the 70 tons of bronze (which were set aside for casting the Gran Cavallo, but Leonardo did not use them in two years) to be used for cannon to defend the city from invasion by the King of France Charles VIII, 24, (30 June 1470 – 7 April 1498, aged 27.8, King for 14.6 years: 30 Aug 1483 – 7 April 1498).

1495 – Leonardo, 43, was commissioned to paint the mural Il Cenacolo or L'Ultima Cena (The Last Supper) in Milano for the refectory of the Convent of Santa Maria delle Grazie – finished after 3 years, in 1498. It is the most reproduced religious painting of all time.

He also started painting the second Madonna of the Rocks (or the Virgin of the Rocks) – this is the second of the two different paintings, which are almost identical – finished after 13 years, in 1508, and he took it to France. The first was painted 12 years earlier, in 1483.

His mother Caterina, 63, died.

Michelangelo, 20, returned to Florence, and carved St. John the Baptist, and the Sleeping Cupid for Lorenzo di Pierfrancesco de' Medici.

1496 – Leonardo was 44 when his half-brother Guglielmo da Vinci was born, his father being 69.
Leonardo began to study mathematics under Luca Pacioli, 49, and prepared a series of drawings of regular solids in a skeletal form, to be engraved as plates for Pacioli's book "De divina proportione", published in 1509.

Michelangelo was 21 when Cardinal Raffaele Riario, 35, (3 May 1461 – 9 July 1521, aged 60.2), to whom Lorenzo had sold St. John the Baptist and the Sleeping Cupid as old sculptures, discovered that they were not old sculptures, how he was told, but was so impressed by the quality of the sculptures that he invited Michelangelo to Rome.

25 June – Michelangelo, 21.3, arrived in Rome.

4 July - He began work on a commission for Cardinal Raffaele Riario, an over-life-size statue of the Roman wine god Bacchus. Upon completion one year later, the work was rejected by the cardinal, and subsequently entered the collection of the banker Jacopo Galli, for his garden.

1497 – Leonardo was 45 when his half-brother Bartolomeo da Vinci was born, his father being 70.

November - Michelangelo was 22.6 when the French ambassador to the Holy See, Cardinal Jean de Bilhères-Lagraulas, 62, (1435 – 6 August 1499, Rome, aged 64, buried in the Chapel of

St. Petronilla in St. Peter's Basilica), commissioned him to carve a Pietà, a sculpture showing the Virgin Mary grieving over the body of Jesus, for the Chapel of St. Petronilla, the chapel of the King of France in St. Peter's Basilica in Vatican.

1498 – Leonardo was 46 when his half-brother Giovanni da Vinci was born, his father being 71. In all, Leonardo had 16 half-siblings, twelve half-siblings from his father, who were much younger than he was (the last was born when Leonardo was 46 years old), and four half-siblings from his mother (younger but closer to his age) - with all of them he had very few contacts.

7 April – Death of the King of France Charles VIII, aged 27.8, (30 June 1470 – 7 April 1498, King for 14.6 years: 30 Aug 1483 – 7 April 1498).

The new King of France is Louis XII, 35.8, (27 June 1462 – 1 Jan 1515, aged 52.5, King for 16.7 years: 7 April 1498 – 1 Jan 1515).

August – Michelangelo was 23.4 when the contract for Pietà was agreed upon, and he began to carve the Rome Pietà.

1499 – 6 September - Leonardo was 47.4 when Ludovico Sforza, 47.2, was overthrown in the Second Italian War (1499 – 1504) by the King of France Louis XII, 37.2, who becomes the new Duke of Milan for 12.7 years: 6 Sep 1499 – 16 June 1512.

At the start of the Second Italian War in 1499, the invading French troops used the life-size clay model for the Gran Cavallo, for target practice.

Leonardo, with his assistant Salai, 19, (Gian Giacomo Caprotti da Oreno, better known as Salaì (1480 – 19 Jan 1524, aged 44), Italian artist and pupil of Leonardo da Vinci for 28 years, from 1490 (age 10) to 1518 (age 38); he painted under the name Andrea Salai), and with his friend, the mathematician Luca Pacioli (Fra Luca Bartolomeo de Pacioli, 52, (c. 1447 – 1517, aged 70), Italian mathematician, Franciscan friar, collaborator with Leonardo da Vinci, and an early contributor to the field now known as accounting. He is referred to as "The Father of Accounting and Bookkeeping", and he was the first person to publish a work on the double-entry system of book-keeping), fled Milan for Venice, where he was employed as a military architect and engineer, devising methods to defend the city from naval attack, using a system of moveable barricades.

The Doge of Venice was Agostino Barbarigo, 80, (3 June 1419 – 20 Sep 1501, aged 82.3, Doge for 15 years: 1486 – 1501). In 1499 started the Ottoman (under sultan Bayezid II) – Venetian War, for 4 years, until 1503.

Michelangelo was 24 when the completed Pietà, one of the world's great masterpieces of sculpture, which is now located in St. Peter's Basilica in Vatican.

Michelangelo returned to Florence, now under the government of Piero Soderini, 49, (18 May 1450 – 13 June 1522, aged 72, Ruler for 14 years: 1498 - 1512).

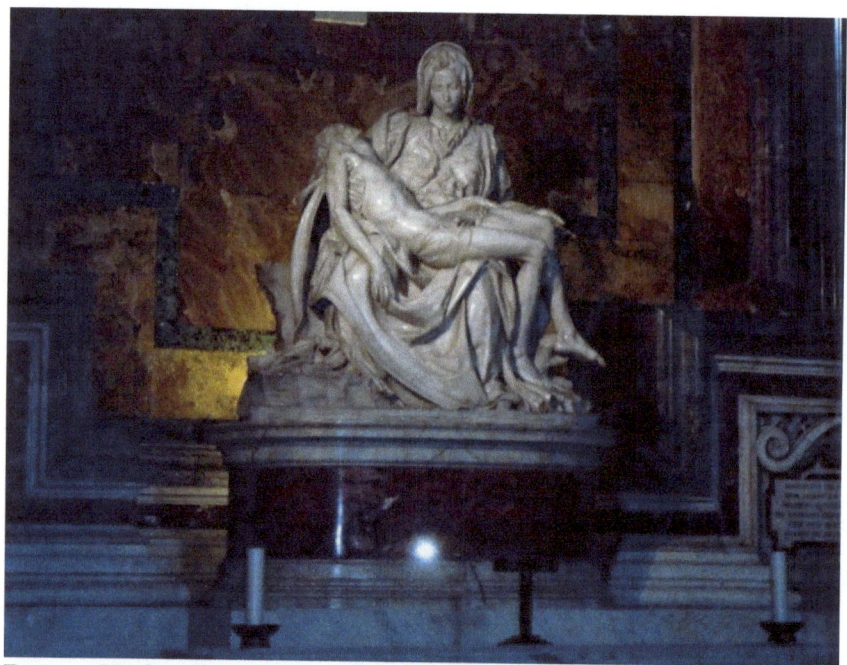

Rome, Vatican, Basilica di San Pietro (1506): the sculpture in Carrara marble Pietà (1498–1499, moved to the first chapel on the right around 1750) by Michelangelo Buonarroti (1475 – 1564). It is the only piece Michelangelo ever signed.

1500 – Leonardo, 48, sketches the design for a machine gun, and painted Salvator Mundi (which was sold, after 517 years, for a world record $450.3 M at a Christie's auction in New York, on 15 November 2017, the highest price ever paid for a work of art).

He returned to Florence, and, together with his assistants, were guests of the Servite monks at the monastery of Santissima Annunziata, and were provided with a workshop, where, Leonardo created the full-size cartoon of The Virgin and Child with St Anne and St John the Baptist, a work that won much admiration, now at National Gallery in London.

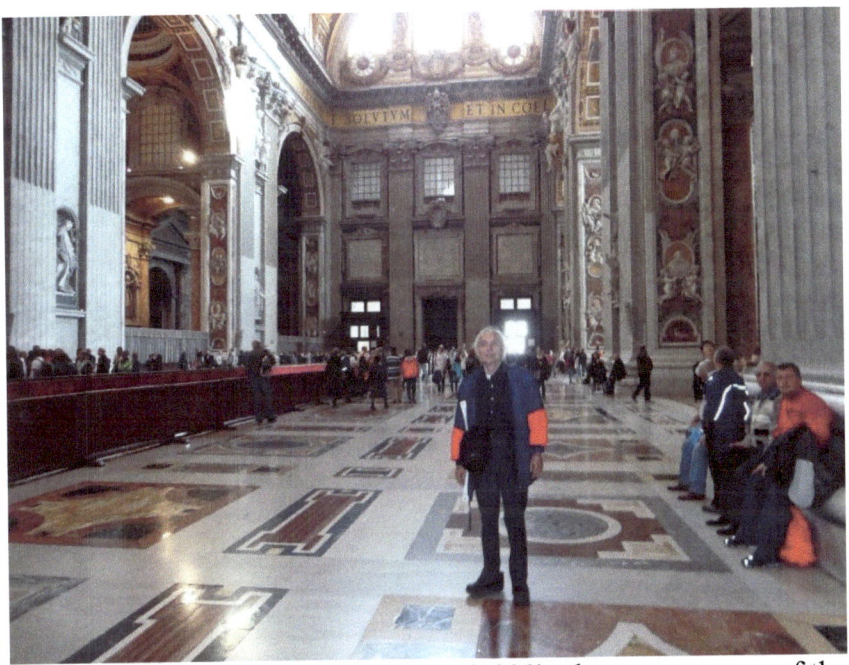

Rome (753 BC), Vatican City State (1929): the eastern nave of the Basilica di San Pietro (1506 – 1626,), designed by Michelangelo and finished by Maderno, the entrance is in the back.

1501 – Michelangelo, 26, contracted to carve Madonna and Child for the Piccolomini altar, and received the commission, from the consuls of the Guild of Wool, to complete an unfinished project begun 40 years earlier, in 1460, by Agostino di Duccio (1418 – 1481, aged 63, Italian sculptor): a colossal statue of Carrara marble portraying David as a symbol of Florentine freedom, to be placed on the gable of Florence Cathedral. Michelangelo responded by starting to work on this statue for 3 years, completing his most famous work, the statue of David, in 1504.

1502 – Leonardo, 50, was in Cesena (city 15 km west of the Adriatic Sea, 30 km northwest of San Marino, and 90 km northeast of Firenze), and entered the service of Cesare Borgia, 27, (13 Sep 1475 – 12 March 1507, aged 31.5, Italian nobleman, politician and cardinal), the son of Pope Alexander VI, 71, (1 Jan 1431 – 18 August 1503, aged 72.6, Pope for 11 years: 11 August 1492 – 18 August 1503) with his mistress Vannozza dei Cattanei, 60, (13 July 1442 – 24 Nov 1518, aged 76.3). Cesare Borgia briefly employed Leonardo da Vinci as military architect and engineer between 1502 and 1503. Cesare provided Leonardo with an unlimited pass to inspect and direct all ongoing and planned construction in his domain. Leonardo built the canal (15 km) from Cesena to the Porto Cesenatico, on the Adriatic Sea. He created a map of Cesare Borgia's stronghold, a town plan of Imola (50 km northwest of Cesena, and 30 km southeast of Bologna) in order to win his patronage. Upon seeing it, Cesare hired Leonardo as his chief military engineer and architect. Later in the year, Leonardo produced another map for his patron, one of Val di Chiana (Chiana Valley, 70 km southeast of Firenze, south of Arezzo, best seen from Cortona, looking west), Toscana.

Leonardo sketches the design for the Golden Horn Bridge – a single span 240 m bridge over the Horn (a prominent body of water, horn-shaped estuary, that joins Bosphorus Strait at the immediate point where the strait meets the Sea of Marmara, thus forming to the south a narrow, isolated peninsula, the tip of which is "Old ancient Byzantium and Constantinople, now Istanbul". Leonardo produced this drawing of a single span bridge as part of a civil engineering project for Ottoman Sultan Beyazid II of Constantinople. The bridge was intended to span an inlet at the mouth of the Bosporus known as the Golden Horn. Beyazid did not pursue the project, because he believed that such a construction was impossible. Leonardo's vision was resurrected in 2001, when a smaller bridge based on his design was constructed in Norway.

Michelangelo, 27, carved in shallow relief The Taddeo Tondo, which shows the Christ Child frightened by a Bullfinch, a symbol of the Crucifixion.

1503 – Leonardo, 51, returned to Florence, and started painting in oil on a poplar panel the Mona Lisa (or La Gioconda) – finished after 3 years, in 1506. It is the most famous portrait, now at Louvre Museum, Paris, France. After 457 years, on 8 Jan 1963 this Mona Lisa (or La Gioconda) from Louvre will be exhibited in the United States for the first time, at the National Gallery of Art in Washington, D.C.

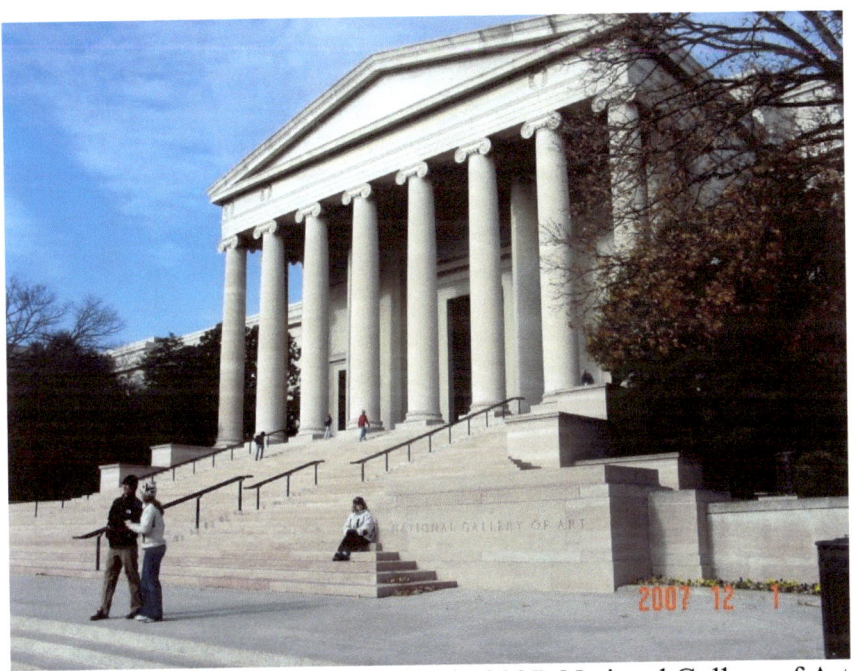

U. S. A., Washington, D.C. (1790) in 2007, National Gallery of Art (1937, in the National Mall).

18 October - He rejoined the Guild of Saint Luke (for painters and other artists) and worked two years designing and painting a mural of The Battle of Anghiari for the Signoria (the council chamber of the Palazzo Vecchio, depicting the battle between Florence and Milan in 1440).

Michelangelo, 28, painted for one year Madonna and Child with John the Baptist, now in the National Gallery, London. He was commissioned Twelve Apostles for the Florence Cathedral, but only completed a portion of St. Matthew.

Michelangelo was commissioned by Angelo Doni to paint a "Holy Family", as a present for his wife, Maddalena Strozzi. It is known as the Doni Tondo and hangs in the Uffizi Gallery in its original splendid frame, which Michelangelo may have designed.

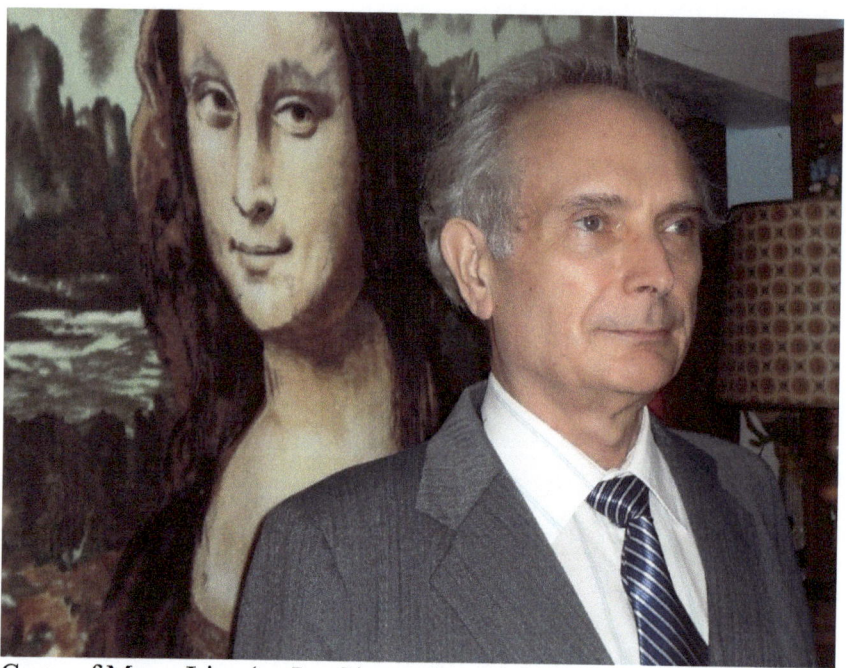

Copy of Mona Lisa (or La Gioconda), 1506, by Leonardo da Vinci

1504 – 9 July – Leonardo was 52.2 when his father, Piero da Vinci, passes away at 77.

Michelangelo, 29, completed the statue of David, and received commission to paint the Battle of Cascina, on the opposite wall from Leonardo's Battle of Anghiari - he finished the cartoon but never the fresco. Leonardo depicts soldiers fighting on horseback, while Michelangelo has soldiers being ambushed as they bathe in the river. Neither work was completed, and both were lost when the chamber was refurbished. Both works were much admired, and copies remain of them, Leonardo's work having been copied by Sir Peter Paul Rubens (28 June 1577 – 30 May 1640, aged 62.9, great Flemish painter, father of eight children (3 with his first wife Isabella, and 5 with his second wife Helena)), and Michelangelo's by Bastiano da Sangallo, 23, (1481 – 31 May 1551, aged 70, Italian sculptor and painter, pupil of Perugino).

Michelangelo also completed the statue of Madonna and Child, now in Bruges, Belgium.

He began painting, for 2 years, The Doni Tondo, depicting the Holy Family.

Leonardo and Botticelli, 59, were part of a committee formed to relocate, against Michelangelo's will, his statue of David, from the gable of Florence Cathedral to, ultimately, the Piazza della Signoria, in front of the Palazzo Vecchio. It now stands in the Galleria dell'Accademia di Firenze (1784, 1 km north of Palazzo Vecchio), while a replica occupies its place in the square.

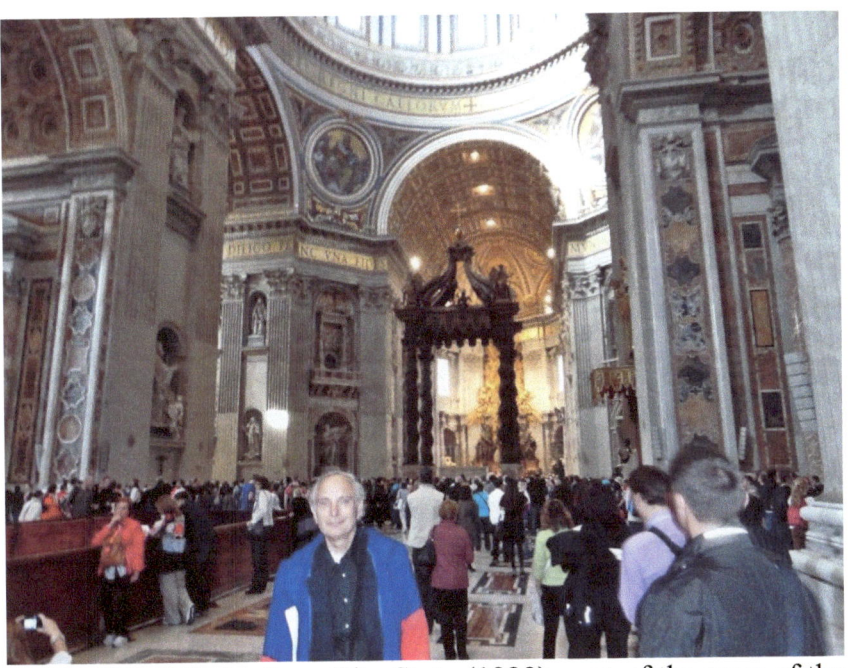

Rome (753 BC), Vatican City State (1929): part of the nave of the Basilica di San Pietro (1506 – 1626,), designed by Michelangelo and finished by Maderno, il baldacchino (center, 30 m, Bernini).

1505 – Leonardo, 53, finished the painted mural The Battle of Anghiari – a lost painting. It was a fresco commissioned for the Salone dei Cinquecento (Hall of the Five Hundred) in the Palazzo Vecchio, Florence.

His Codex on the Flight of Birds, which comprises 18 folios, was finished this year, after 15 years of work.

Michelangelo, 30, was summoned to Rome by Pope Julius II, 61.5, (5 Dec 1443 – 21 Feb 1513, aged 69.2, Pope for 9.3 years: 1 Nov 1503 – 21 Feb 1513), and commissioned to create the tomb for the pope, which was to include forty statues, and be finished in five years. He spent eight months in the quarries of Carrara (100 km northwest of Florence, and 170 km southeast of Milano, on the Carrione River) selecting marble for the tomb.

Raphael, 22, (1483 – 1520, aged 37) painted The Small Cowper Madonna.

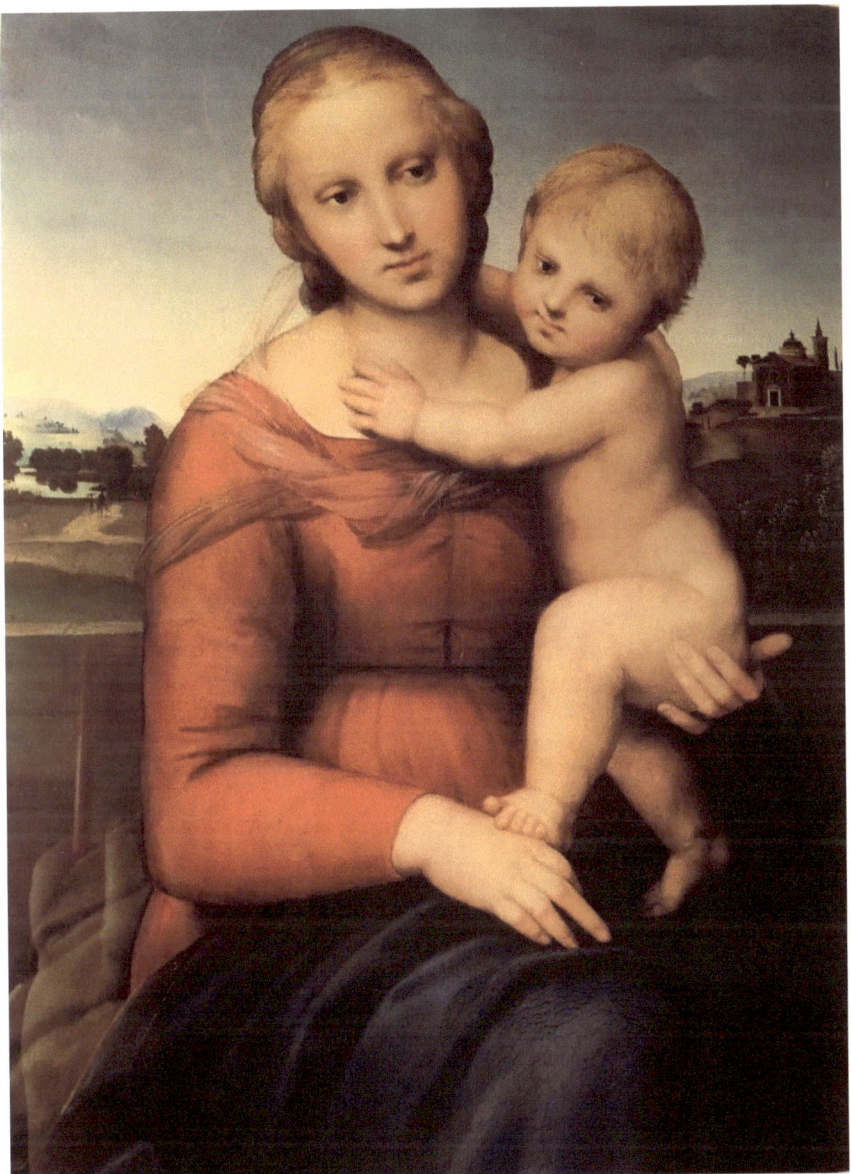

Raphael, 22, 1505, (1483 – 1520, aged 37) painted The Small Cowper Madonna, at the National Gallery of Art in Washington, D.C.

Under the patronage of the pope, Michelangelo experienced constant interruptions to his work on the tomb in order to accomplish numerous other tasks. Then, for 40 years, until 1545,

Michelangelo worked on the tomb of Julius II on and off, in both Rome and Florence, carved the central figure of Moses (1516), the Rebellious Slave (1513, 2.15 m high marble statue, now in the Louvre in Paris) and Dying Slave (1513 - 1516, 2.15 m high marble statue, now in the Louvre in Paris), Rachel, and Leah. The tomb of Pope Julius II is located now in the Church of San Pietro in Vincoli (439, 3.2 km east of Basilica San Pietro in Vatican (where initially it was supposed to be, Donato Bramante, 61, (1444 – 11 April 1514, aged 70, Italian architect, was working on the building), 400 m north of Amphitheatrum Flavium (Colosseum)) in Rome.

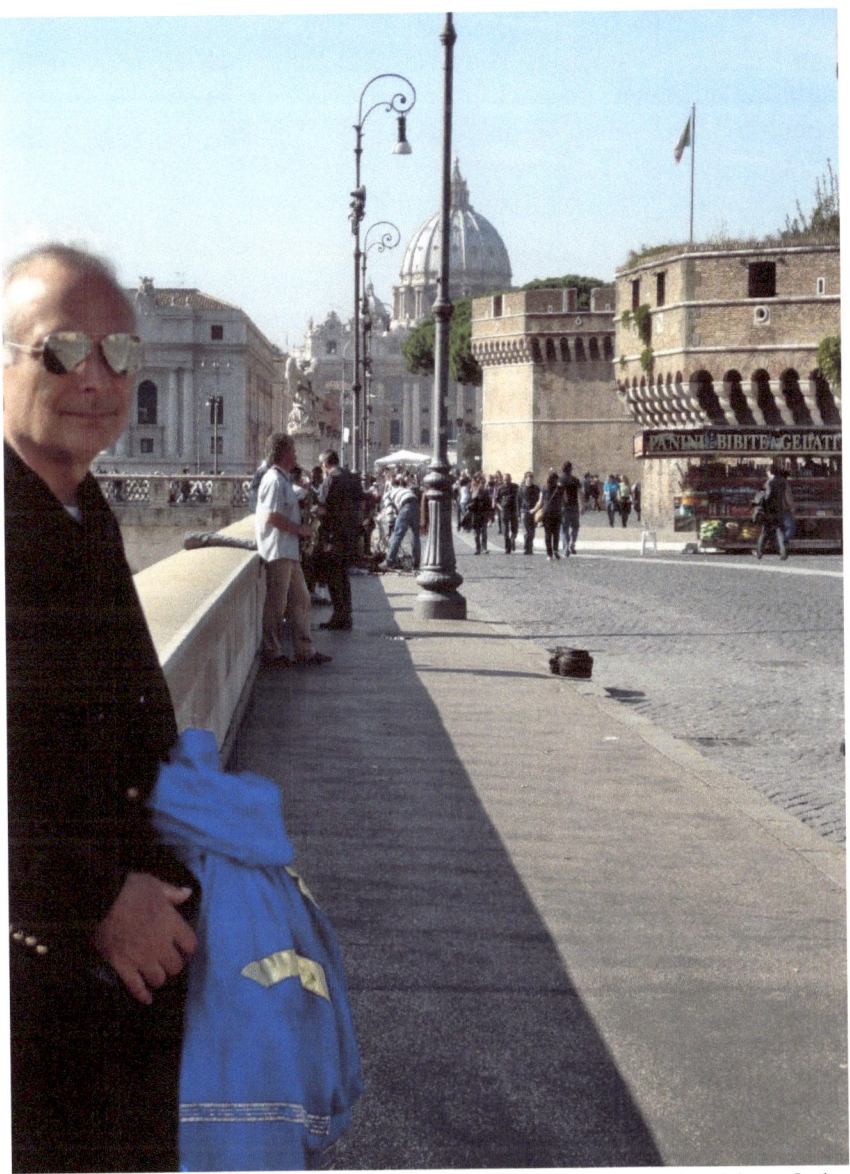

Rome (753 BC): from Lungotevere Prati, the south side of the Mausoleum (right, 135-139) of Hadrian (76–138, Emperor 117-138, renamed Castel Sant'Angelo in 600), and part of the east side of the Basilica di San Pietro (center, 1506 – 1626,), designed by Michelangelo and finished by Maderno.

1506 – Leonardo, 54, returned to Milan, where many of his pupils or followers in painting either knew or worked with him, including Bernardino Luini, Giovanni Antonio Boltraffio and Marco d'Oggiono. At this time he probably commenced a project for an equestrian figure of Charles II d'Amboise, the acting French governor of Milan. A wax model survives and, if genuine, is the only extant example of Leonardo's sculpture.

April - Michelangelo, 31, returned to Florence, and the Tomb project was put on hold.

November - Michelangelo and Pope Julius II reconciled in Bologna.

The foundations of St. Peter's Basilica in Rome had been laid to the plans of Bramante. Forty years later, in 1546, Michelangelo will be appointed architect of this St. Peter's Basilica.

1507 – Leonardo, 55, was back in Florence working with his half-brothers over his father's estate.

1508 – Leonardo, 56, was back in Milano, living in his own house in Porta Orientale in the parish of Santa Babila, and he painted (for about 2 years) in oil the Virgin and Child with St. Anne (the mother of Virgin Mary), now at Louvre Museum, Paris, France.

27 May - Ludovico Sforza died at 55.8 (27 July 1452 – 27 May 1508).

February - Michelangelo, 32.9, returned to Florence, but he was summoned to Rome by Pope Julius II, 64.2, and asked to paint the ceiling of the Sistine Chapel, which he finished after 4.6 years, in October 1512. Michelangelo was originally commissioned to paint the Twelve Apostles on the triangular pendentives that supported the ceiling, and to cover the central part of the ceiling with ornament. Michelangelo persuaded Pope Julius II to give him a free hand, and proposed a different and more complex scheme, representing the Creation, the Fall of Man, the Promise of Salvation through the prophets, and the genealogy of Christ. The work is part of a larger scheme of decoration within the chapel.

Birth of Andrea Palladio (1508-1580, aged 72) important Italian architect.

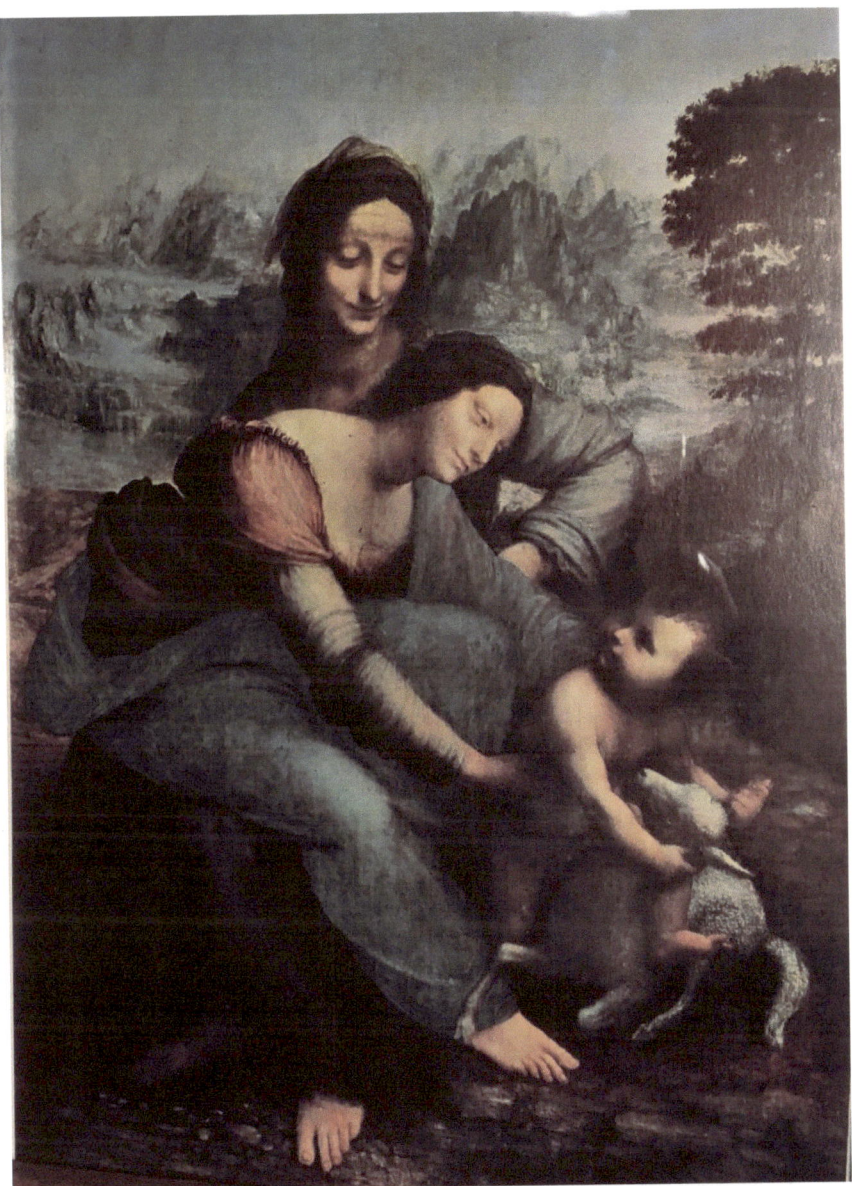

Leonardo da Vinci, 56, 1508, The Virgin and Child with St. Anne

1509 – Leonardo, 57, prepared a series of drawings of regular solids in a skeletal form, to be engraved as plates for Pacioli's book "De divina proportione", published in this year.

Michelangelo, 34, completed Ignudo fresco on the Sistine Chapel ceiling.

1510 – Leonardo, 58, collaborated with the doctor Marcantonio della Torre on his work of theoretical anatomy – until 1511.

17 May – Death of Sandro Botticelli (1445 – 17 May 1510, aged 65), 7 years older than Leonardo.

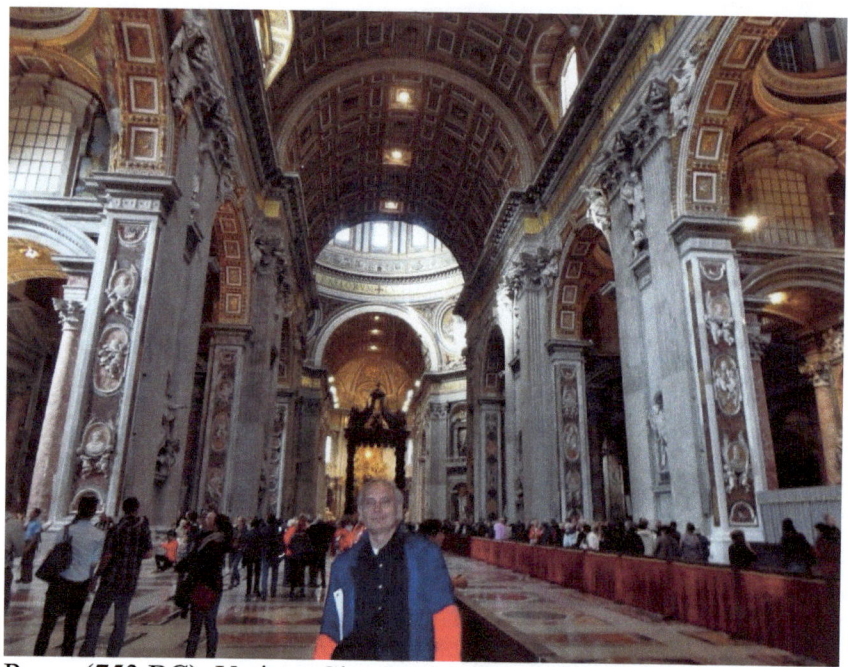

Rome (753 BC), Vatican City State (1929): the nave of the Basilica di San Pietro (1506 – 1626,), designed by Michelangelo and finished by Maderno, il baldacchino (center, 30 m, Bernini).

Michelangelo, 35, completed David and Goliath (1508-1510), fresco vault of the Sistine Chapel. There is a striking pictorial unity between these two figures. David raises his sword to sever the giant's head. Goliath twists around to avoid the blow. Both figures are somewhat foreshortened. David's slingshot, with which he has stunned the giant, lies on the ground in front of Goliath. Michelangelo uses the pendentive form effectively to enclose these figures. Above David, the pink triangle of the tent reverses the architectural form; emphasizing David's upward thrusting arm motion. There is dramatic tension in this gesture, but little anger.

Goliath wears a moss green cuirass, trimmed with gold and purple leggings. His white sleeve, rose tunic and olive green mantle help tie together background and foreground colors. The two soldiers at the top, right, are incidental to the scene. David and Goliath were in the part of the Sistine Ceiling Michelangelo painted first, yet even at this early stage the artist succeeded in realizing his dramatic purpose in a rather tight space.

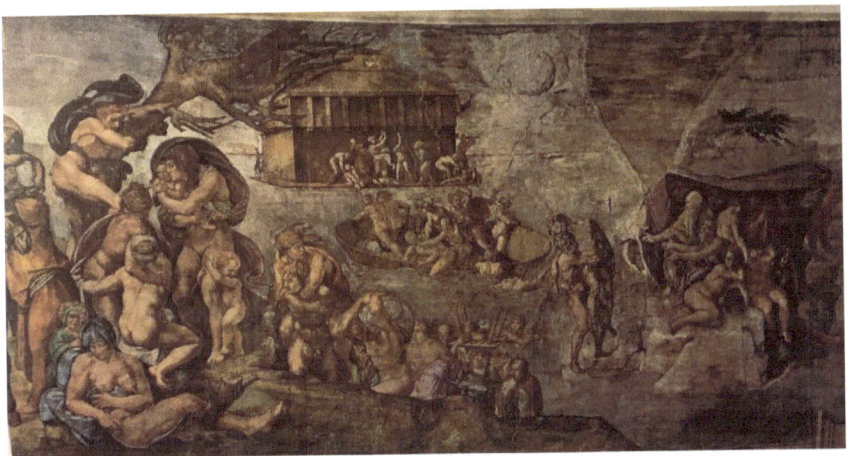

Michelangelo, 35, completed The Deluge (1508-1510), fresco vault of the Sistine Chapel. Michelangelo depicts mankind's flight from destruction, not the storm itself. The most crowded episode on the ceiling, this scene is on three different visual planes. The nearest group, on the left, has climbed to the highest point. The group on the right rests on a rocky ledge as the waters rise. The background figures in the small, overloaded boat, is heading towards the ark. Each group is isolated. The figures at the left show the great effort needed to arrive at this temporary refuge.

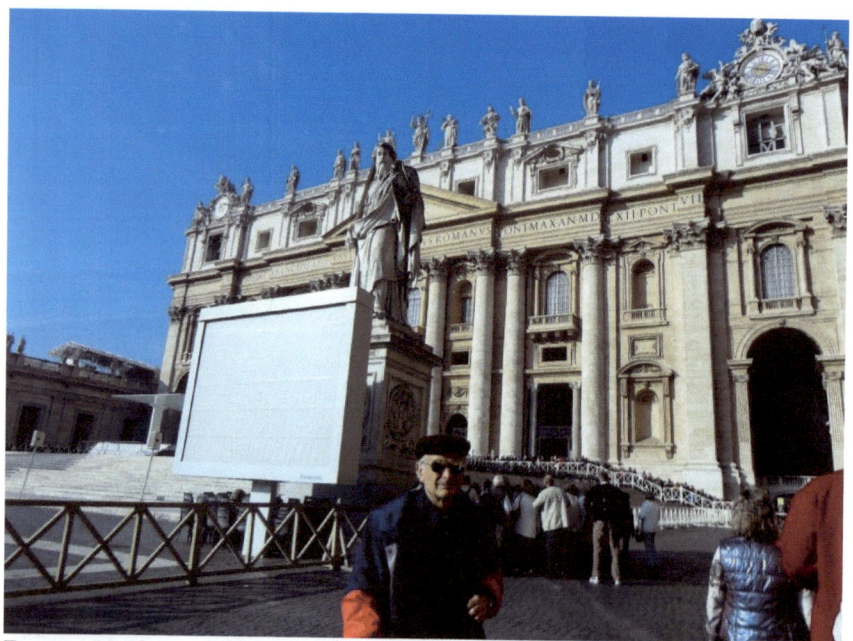

Roma, Vatican, in 2011: Piazza San Pietro (1667, by Gian Lorenzo Bernini): Basilica di San Pietro (1506, by Donato Bramante (1444-1514), Michelangelo (1475-1564), Raphael (1483-1520), Carlo Maderno (1556-1629) and Gian Lorenzo Bernini (1598-1680)).

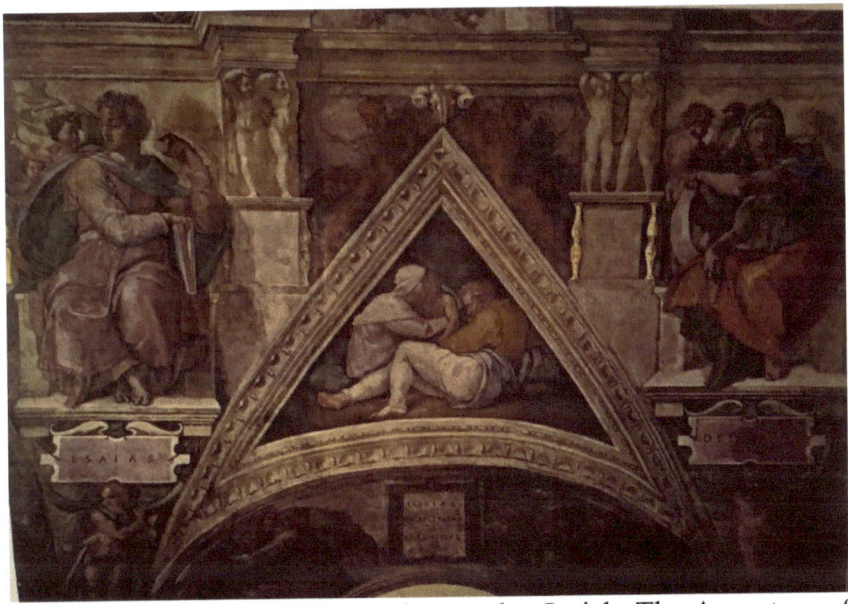

Michelangelo, 35, completed The Prophet Isaiah, The Ancestors of Christ, The Delphic Sibyl (1508-1510), fresco vault of the Sistine Chapel. At the left, a meditative Isaiah turns and listens to the cherub whispering in his year. This figure represents God's voice telling of the coming of the Messiah. In the middle, in one of the eight triangles between the Sibyls and the Prophets, are two of the ancestors of Christ. The man is withdrawn, while the mother protectively shelters her child.

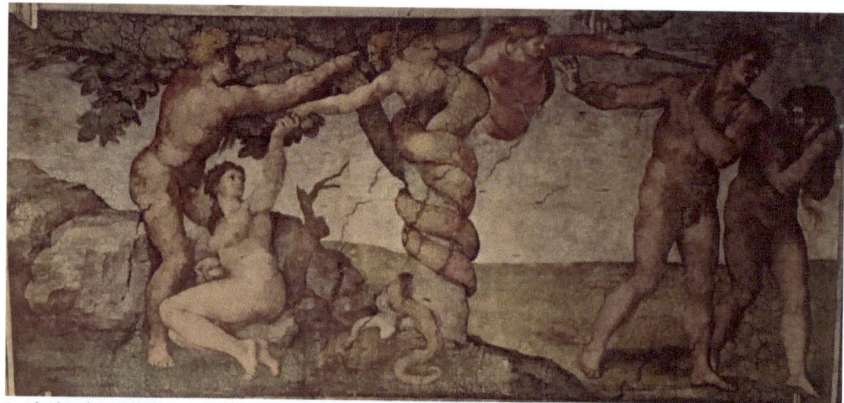

Michelangelo, 35, completed also The Temptation and The Expulsion (1509-1510), fresco vault of the Sistine Chapel. He used the tree of knowledge to separate the two dramatic episodes in the Garden of Eden panel. Eve has a seductive gesture, reaching upward for the fruit. Adam is grasping the limb with his left hand, while reaching with his right. Then, at the right, the thrust of the punishing angel's arm is repeated in Adam's arm reaching back toward off the judgment. The rocky landscape is harsh, and the only sign of vegetation is the leafy limb Adam holds.

1511 – 30 July - Leonardo was 59.3 when Giorgio Vasari was born (30 July 1511 – 27 June 1574, aged 62.9), Italian painter, architect, writer, and historian, most famous today for his "Lives of the Most Excellent Painters, Sculptors, and Architects", considered the foundation of art-historical writing.

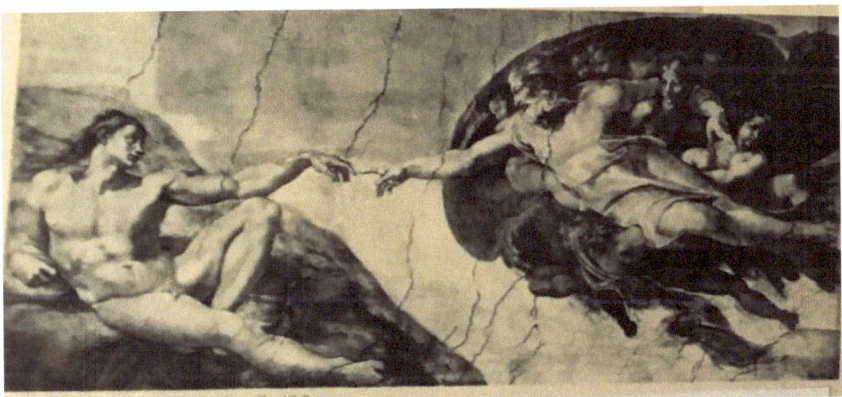

Michelangelo, 36, completed The Creation of Man (1510-1511), a fresco on the vault of the Sistine Chapel. The Lord's gesture is superb, as His mighty arm becomes the channel for the life force. Adam's arm resting passively on his knee. These two figures are the best known of all Sistine paintings.

1512 – October - Michelangelo, 37.6, finished painting the ceiling of the Sistine Chapel in Rome. The composition stretches over 500 m^2 of ceiling, and contains over 300 figures. At its center are nine episodes from the Book of Genesis, divided into three groups: God's creation of the earth; God's creation of humankind and their fall from God's grace; and lastly, the state of humanity as represented by Noah and his family. On the pendentives supporting the ceiling are painted twelve men and women who prophesied the coming of Jesus. Among the most famous paintings on the ceiling are The Creation of Adam, Adam and Eve in the Garden of Eden, the Deluge, the Prophet Jeremiah, and the Cumaean Sibyl.

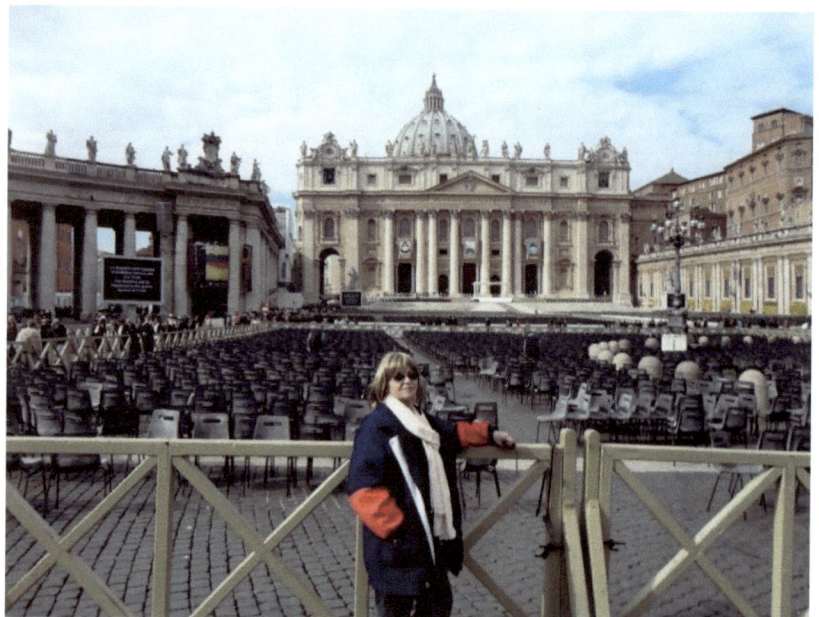

Vatican in 2011: St. Peter's Square (1667), Basilica Papale di San Pietro in Vaticano (1506, center, 138 m height, by Michelangelo).

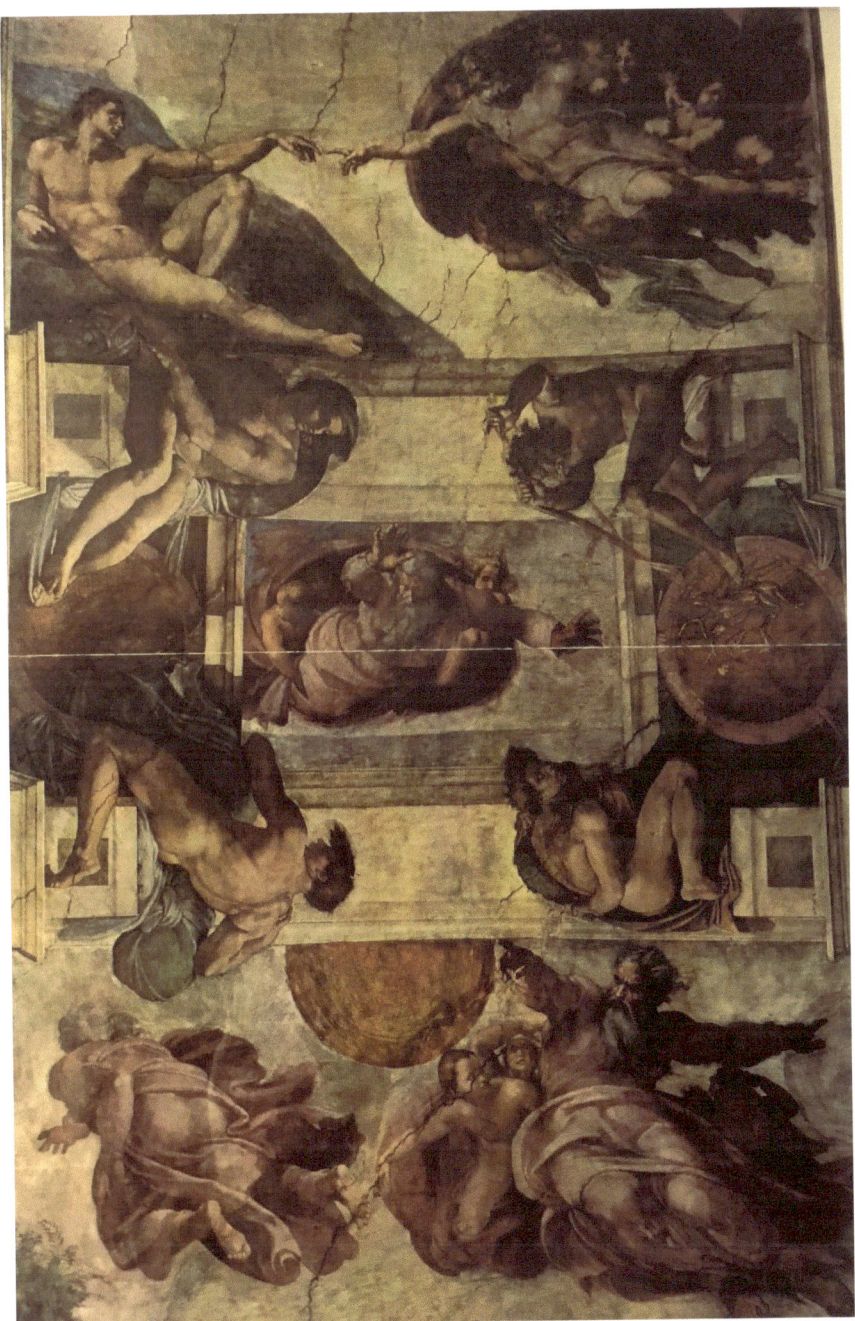

The Creation was painted between 1510 and 1512 – it is a fresco vault of the Sistine Chapel. The creation of the Sun and the Moon (at bottom) was executed first in this group. At the right, the figure of the Lord surges upward and with His imperious right hand assigns the Sun to its place, then with His left, the Moon. Angels attend Him, and one of them shields His eyes from the Sun's brilliance. God's figure hurried away at the left, creating the Earth's vegetation in passing. At the center, borne by angels, God is shown wrapped in a swirling mantle, separating the earth from the waters. In the corners of this section are four powerful, athletic figures (the so called Ignudi), who react to the Lord's actions in varying ways. At the top, in the most famous section, God is enveloped in a shell-like mantle, and, assisted by cherubs, He extends His finger towards Adam. Adam's inert, relaxed body lies in a classic pose, awaiting God's gift of life.

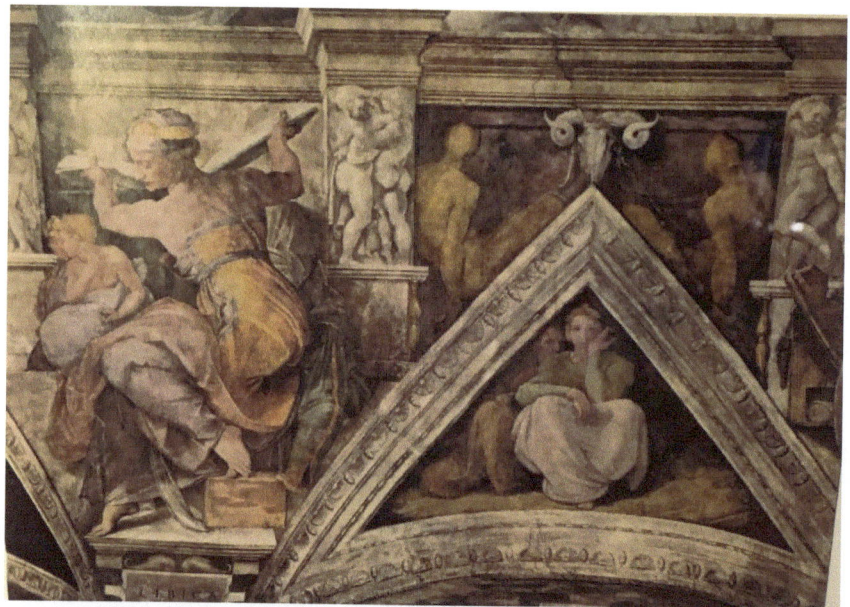

The Libyan Sibyl; The Ancestors of Christ was painted between 1510 and 1512 – it is a fresco vault of the Sistine Chapel. The Libyan Sibyl, lies just below the Lord separating Light from Darkness. One of the cherubs turns away, repeating the profile, and gestures towards the Sibyl.

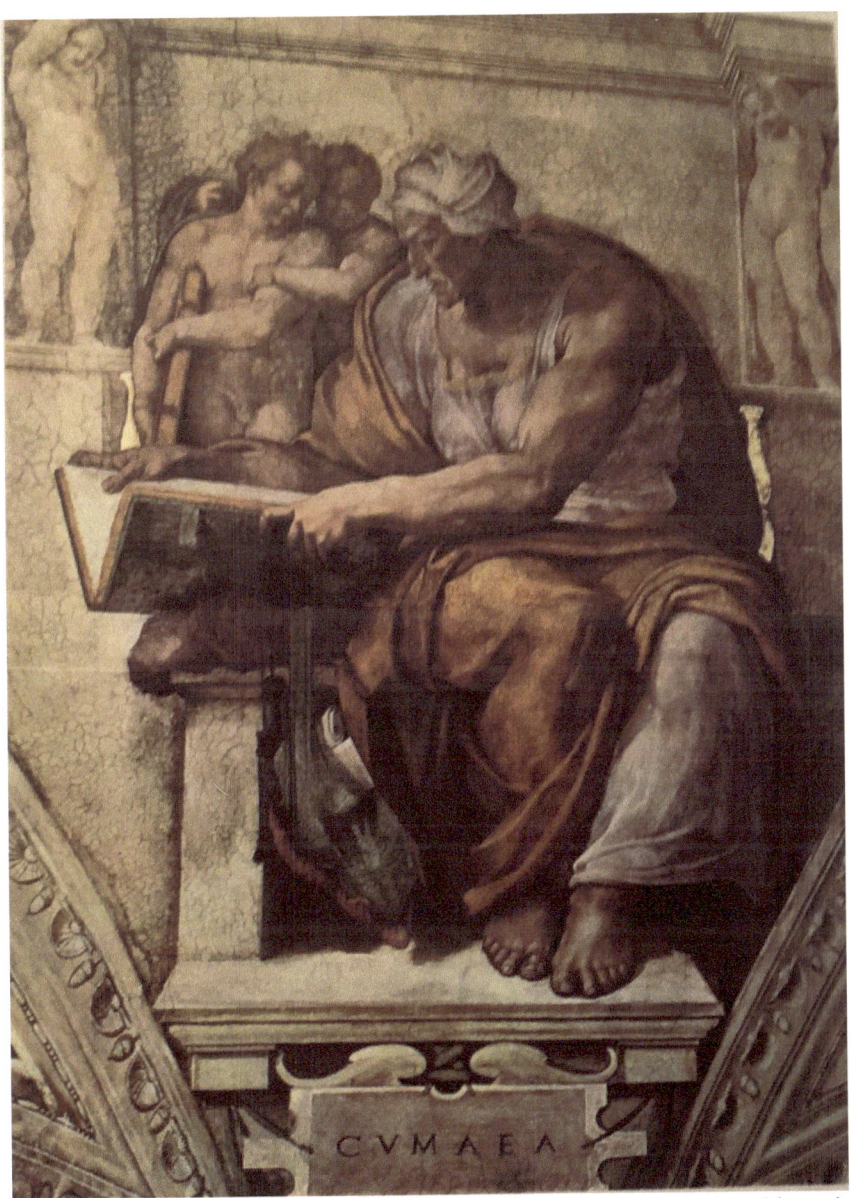

The Cumaean Sibyl (1510-1512), fresco, vault of the Sistine Chapel. Cumaea was the most famous of Apollo's votaries, having sold her three Sibylline books to Tarquin, the last king of early Rome. The descendant of a mythic race of giants, she supposedly foretold the virgin birth of the Redeemer in the fourth of Vergilius's Eclogues. One of the two cherubs at the left brings another book.

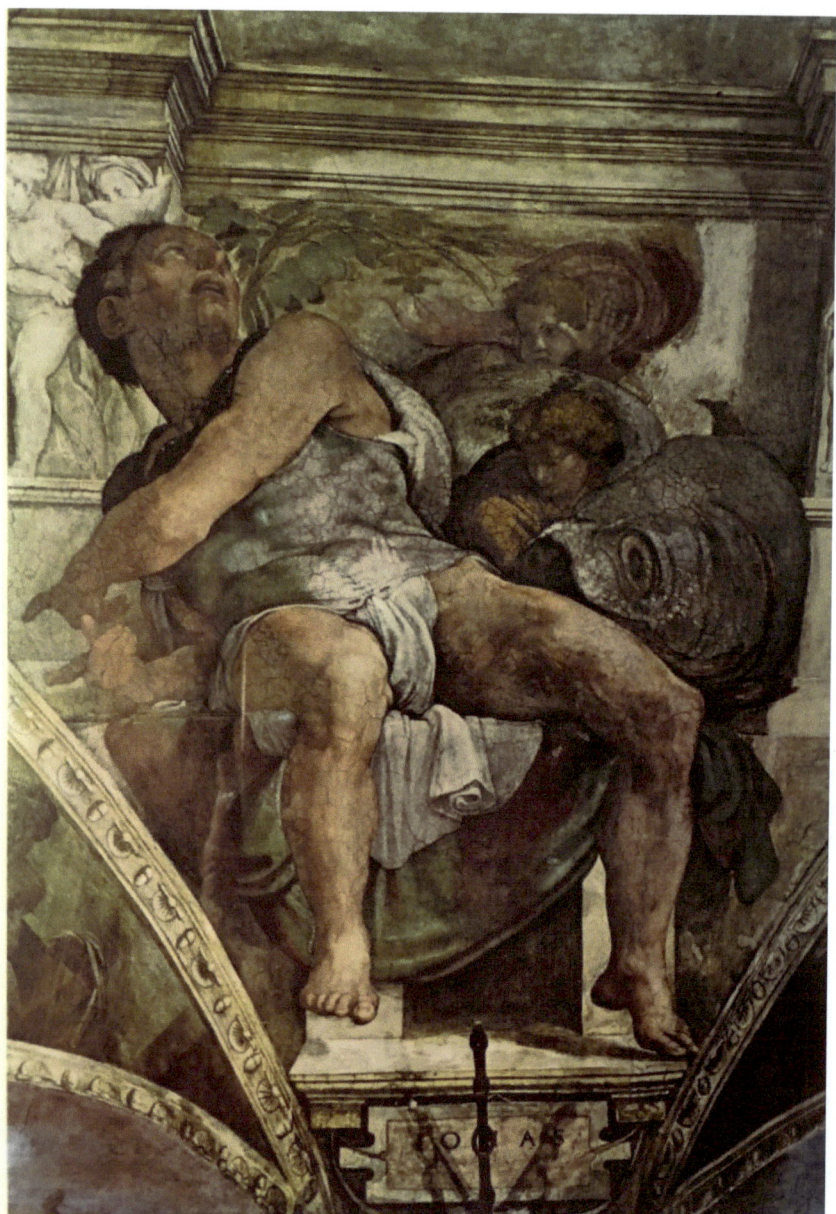

The Prophet Jonah (1510-1512), fresco, vault of the Sistine Chapel. The figure of Jonah, larger than any of the other figures, is situated directly below the depiction of God creating light, and just above the Last Judgement. Rearing backward, he gazes in awe, and dismay at the apparition of God above him. The great fish is placed besides the prophet; behind him is the fig tree.

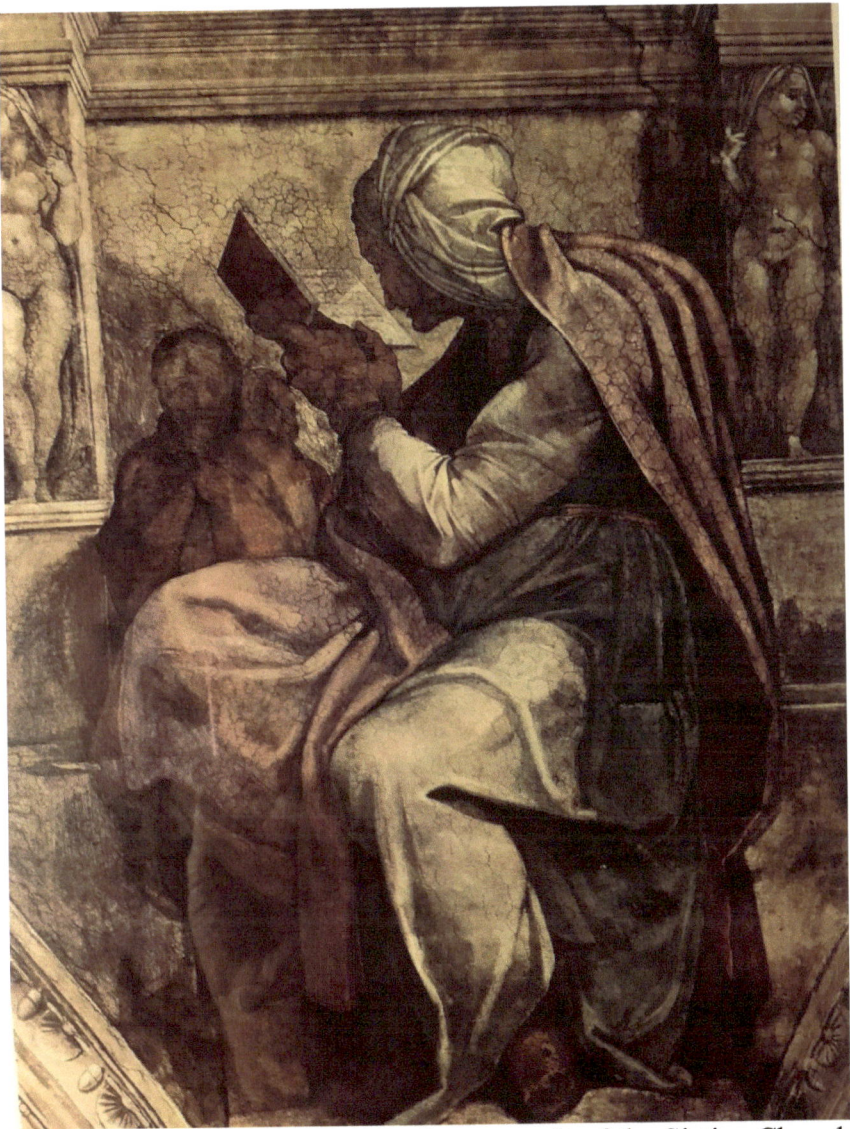

The Persian Sibyl (1510-1512), fresco, vault of the Sistine Chapel. The angel Sibyl is one of the more poignant figures on the Sistine Ceiling. She is seated at an angle; with her head and shoulders turned away to catch the light, as she strains with failing eyesight to read her book of prophecy. Her head is lost in shadow, yet she is clearly very old, with a hump back and gnarled hands. The two attending cherubs are almost hidden in shadow. The Persian Sybil is placed opposite the Prophet Daniel, and together they flank the Creation.

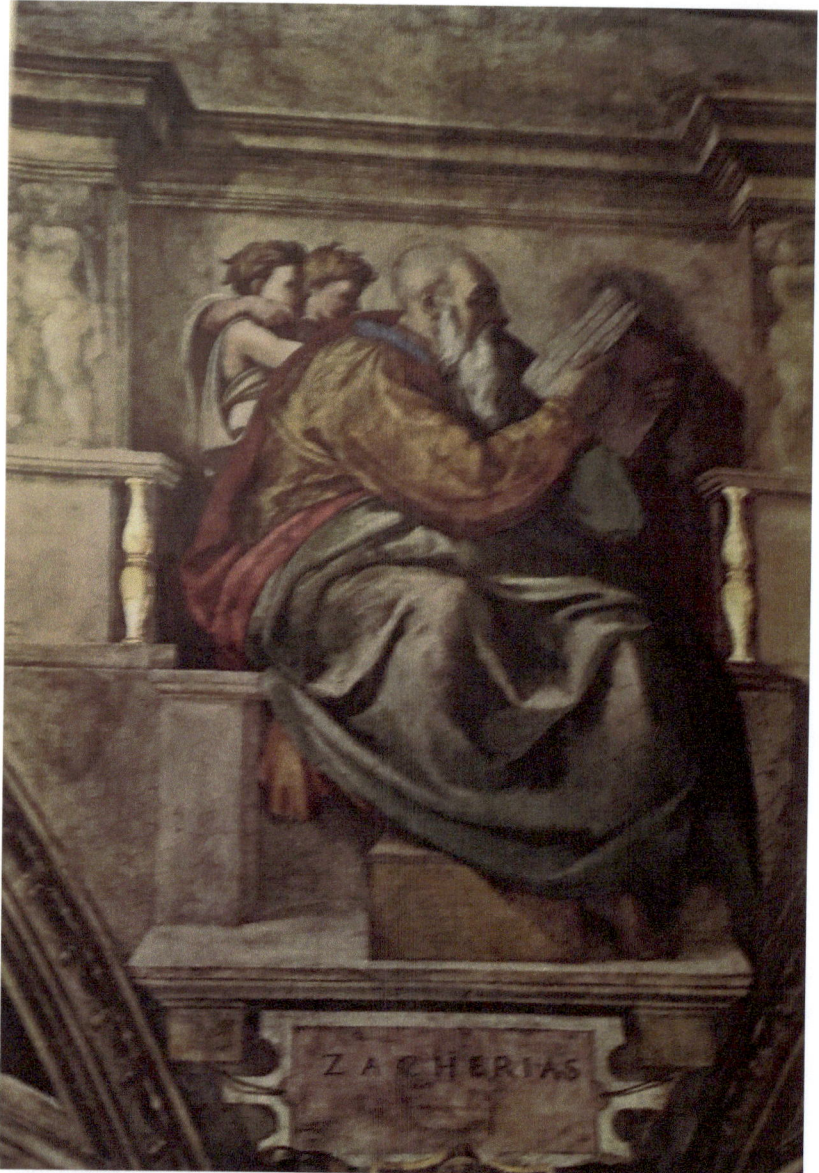

The Prophet Zachariah (1510-1512), fresco, vault of the Sistine Chapel. Zachariah's placement above the entrance to the chapel refers to a coming of Christ, and the events of Palm Sunday. The Pope enters through this doorway on Palm Sunday, after distributing palms to the people. Behind Zachariah are two guardian spirits (genii of cherubs). Zachariah is seated in sharp profile, looking for a particular passage in his book.

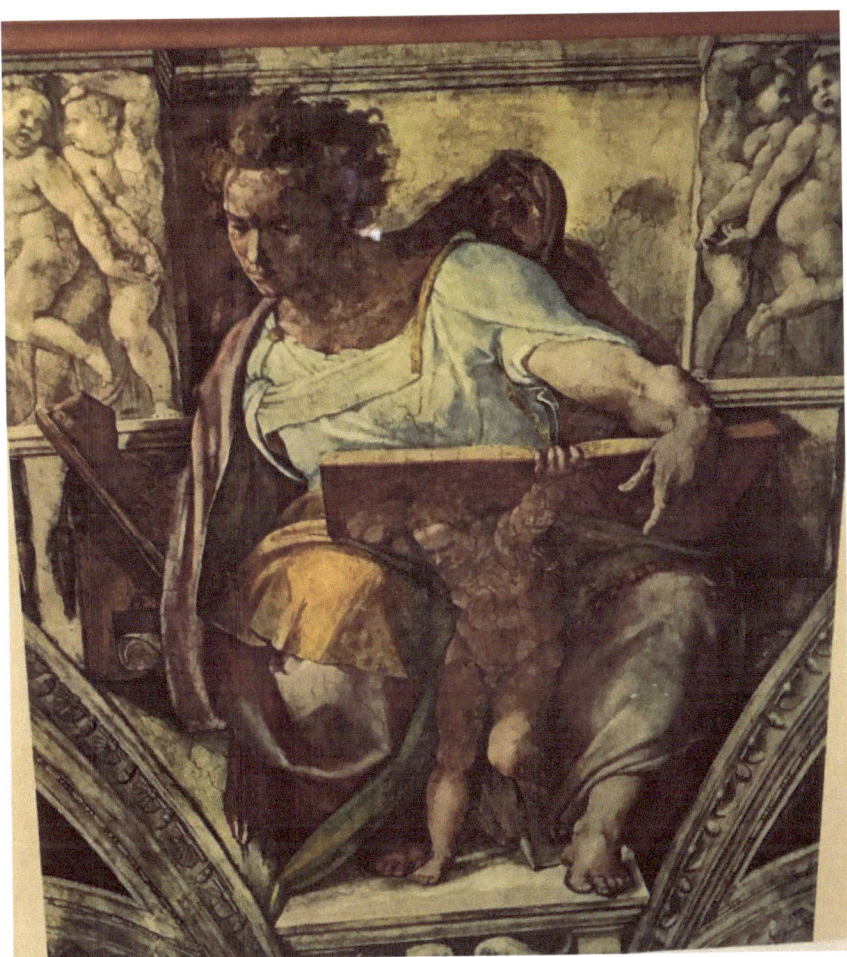

The Prophet Daniel (1510-1512), fresco, vault of the Sistine Chapel. The role of prophets is to announce the coming of Christ. Here Daniel is shown as a young man, holding a large book that rests on the back of a cherub caryatid. The prophet is intent, writing in the tablet, at his left, observations drawn from the book he holds. His expression is serious.

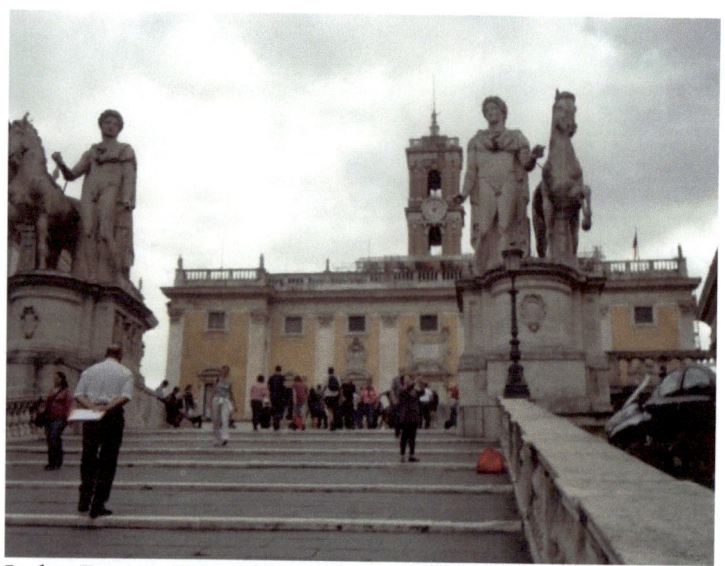

Italy, Rome (753 BC), from cordonata capitolina (flight of steps, which can be also used by horses, with balustrades ending down with two Egyptian lions in black basalt, and up with two marble statues of Castor (left) and Pollux (right), by Michelangelo), Campidoglio (1546 by Michelangelo, on Collis Capitolinus, the oldest part of Rome, with Temple of Jupiter, 509 BC), Palazzo Senatorio (back, 1350, atop Tabularium, now the city hall).

1513 – Leonardo, 61, started the oil painting on walnut wood St. John the Baptist – finished in 1516.

21 February - Michelangelo was 37.9 when Pope Julius II died (5 Dec 1443 – 21 Feb 1513, aged 69.2, Pope for 9.3 years: 1 Nov 1503 – 21 Feb 1513). The Pope's tomb project was revived with a different design - Michelangelo carved Moses and the two Slaves. The Rebellious Slave (1513, 2.15 m high marble statue) is now in the Louvre in Paris.

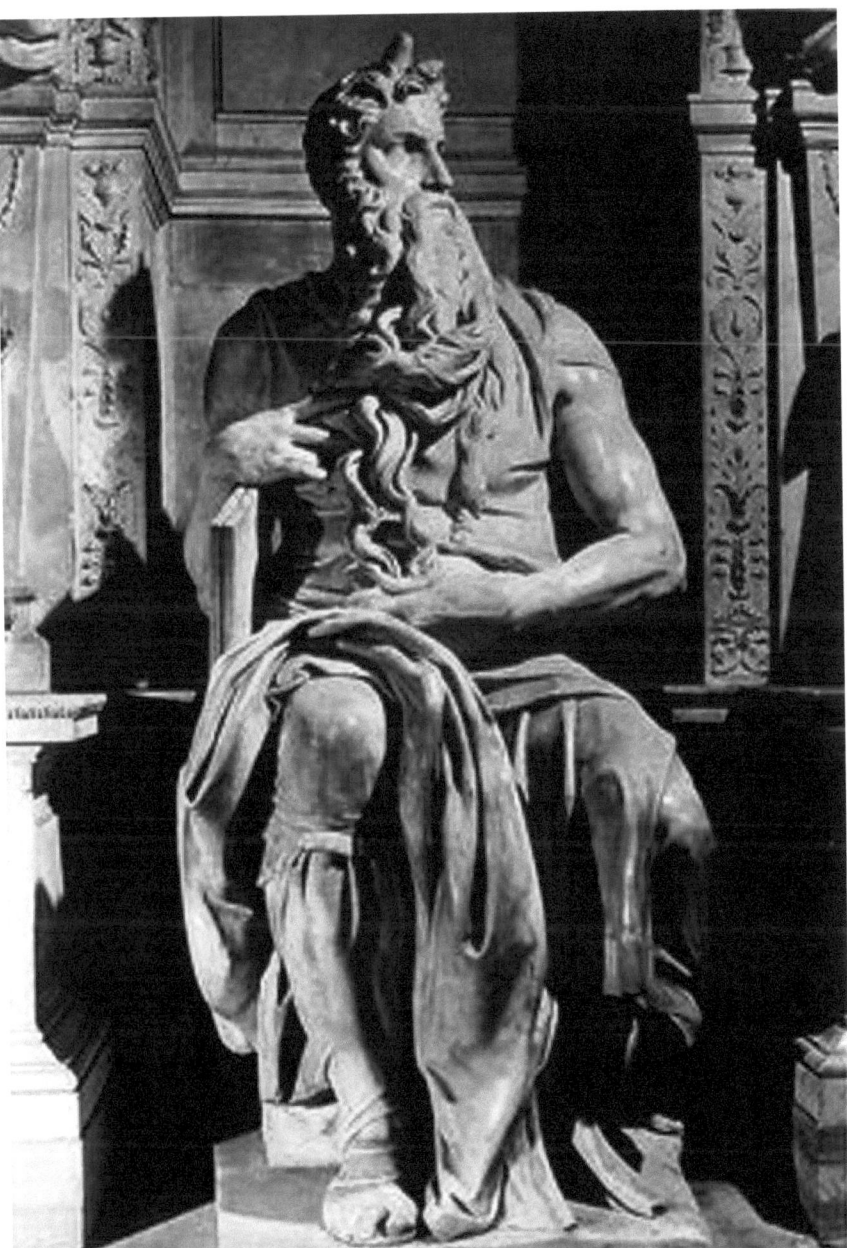

Moses by Michelangelo

9 March – Starts the Papacy of Pope Leo X, 37.2, (11 Dec 1475 – 1 Dec 1521, aged 45.9, Pope for 8.6 years: 9 March 1513 – 1 Dec 1521, the second son of Lorenzo de Medici).

Pope Leo X commissioned Michelangelo to reconstruct the façade of the Basilica of San Lorenzo in Florence, and to adorn it with sculptures. He agreed, and spent three years creating drawings and models for the façade, as well as attempting to open a new marble quarry at Pietrasanta, specifically for the project. After 7 years, in 1520, the work was abruptly cancelled by his financially strapped patrons, before any real progress had been made. The basilica lacks a façade to this day. Michelangelo carved the Dying Slave, now at the Louvre, where Rodin (12 Nov 1840 – 17 Nov 1917, aged 77 years and 5 days), studied the sculpture 350 years later.

From September to 1516, for 3 years, under Pope Leo X, 37.6, Leonardo, 61.4, lived in Il Palazzetto del Belvedere (1484 by Pollaiolo, the Cortile del Belvedere is from 1506, by Donato Bramante, 100 m north of the Cappella Sistina) in the Vatican in Rome, where Raphael, 30, (28 March 1483 – 6 April 1520, aged 37, Italian painter and architect) and Michelangelo, 38, were working.

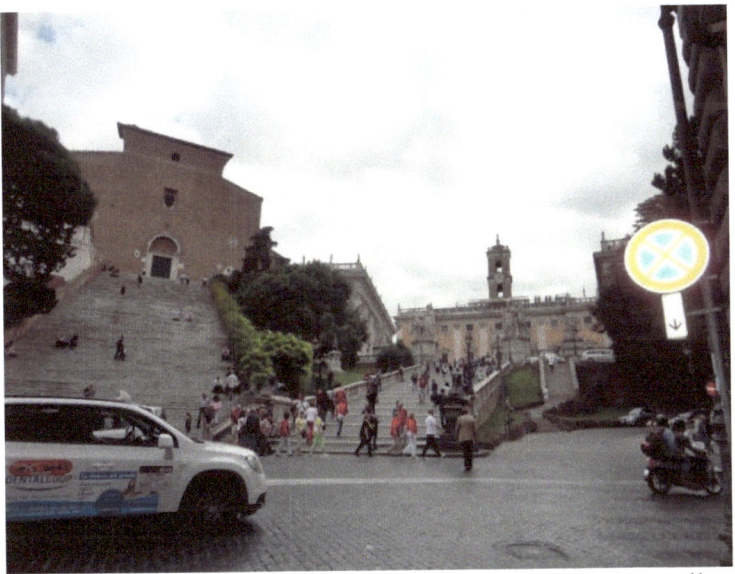

Italy, Rome (753 BC), from Via del Teatro di Marcello at Piazza D'Ara Coeli, Campidoglio (right, 1560 by Michelangelo, on Collis Capitolinus, the oldest part of Rome with Temple of Jupiter, 509 BC), Basilica di Santa Maria in Ara Coeli (Altar of Heaven, left, 1150, 80 m x 45 m, monumental stairway of 124 steps (1348)).

1514 – Michelangelo, 39, began work on Risen Christ.

1515 – 1 January - Leonardo was 62.7 when the King of France Louis XII died at 52.5 (27 June 1462 – 1 Jan 1515, King for 16.7 years: 7 April 1498 – 1 Jan 1515).

The new King of France is Francis I, 20.3, (12 Sep 1494 – 31 March 1547, aged 52.5, King for 32 years and 3 months: 1 Jan 1515 – 31 March 1547).

October - King Francis I, 21.1, of France recaptured Milano.

19 December – Leonardo, 63.6, was present at the meeting of Francis I, 21.2, and Pope Leo X, 40, which took place in Bologna

Leonardo was commissioned to make for Francis a mechanical lion that could walk forward, then open its chest to reveal a cluster of lilies.

Michelangelo, 40, spent 19 years, until 1534, working mostly for the Medici family in Florence. He designed and carved tombs for the family, and also, he designed the Medici Chapel.

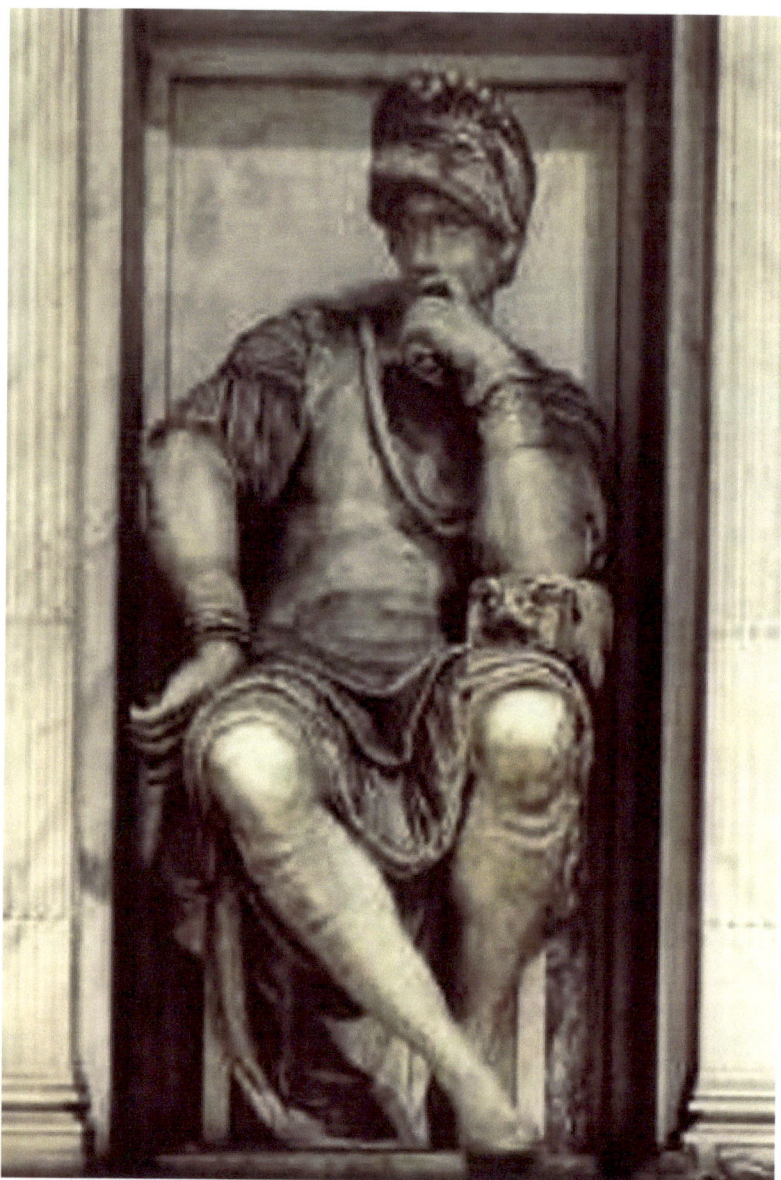

One of de Medici brothers, by Michelangelo.

1516 – Leonardo, 64, entered King Francis' (22) service, being given the use of the manor house Clos Lucé, now a public museum, 500 m southeast of the king's residence at the Château Royal d'Amboise (200 km southwest of Paris). He spent the last three years of his life here, accompanied by his friend and apprentice, Count Francesco Melzi, 25, (c. 1491 – 1568, aged c. 77, Italian painter from a family of the Milanese nobility in Lombardia), and supported by a pension totaling 10,000 scudi/year (about $120,000/year, which was about 50 times the average annual income at that time).

 Michelangelo, 41, finished the central figure of Moses (now in Rome), Dying Slave (1513 - 1516, 2.15 m high marble statue, now in the Louvre in Paris), and was commissioned to design the façade for the Medici family church of St. Lorenzo.

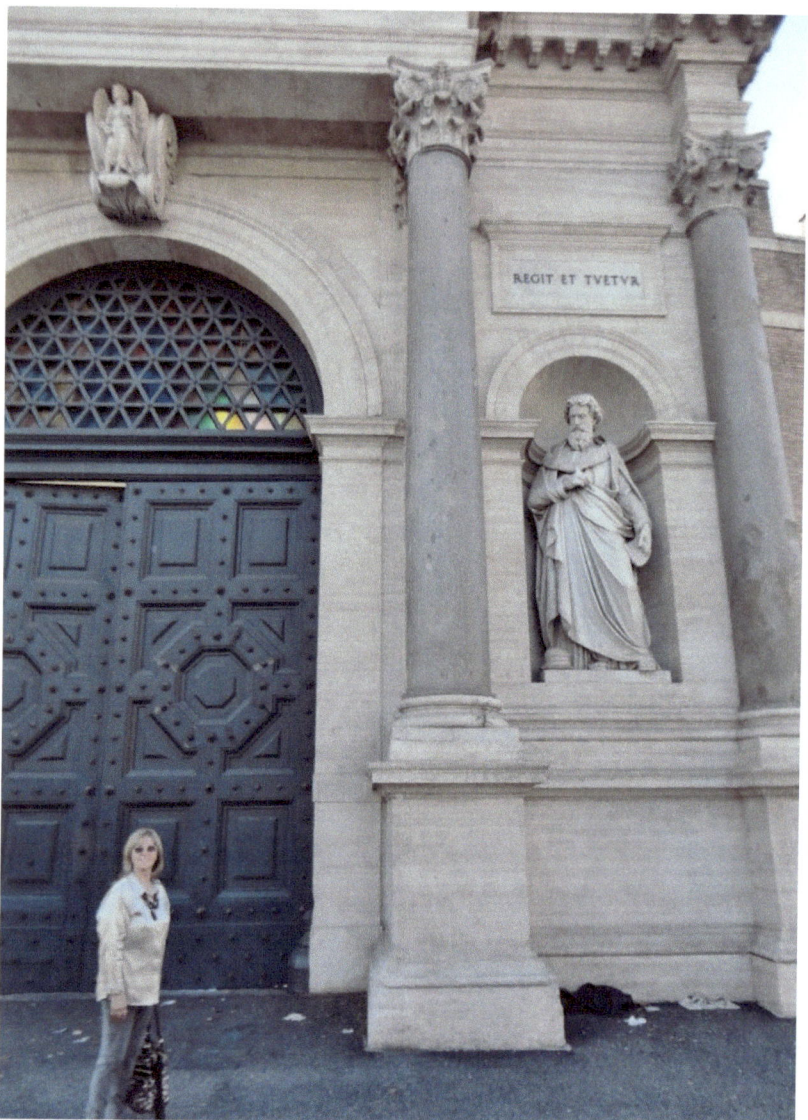

Italy, Rome (753 BC, one of the oldest continuously occupied cities in Europe, called Roma Aeterna (The Eternal City) and Caput Mundi (Capital of the World)), the northeast half of the external façade (1869) of Porta Pia (1565, by Pope Pius IV (1499-1565), designed by Michelangelo (1475-1564), a gate in the Aurelian (214-275) Walls (275) of Rome), with a statue of Saint Alexander, and the inscription REGIT ET TVETVR; on the right and in the back is the seat of Museo Storico dei Bersaglieri.

1517 – Leonard was 65 when his friend the mathematician Luca Pacioli died at the age of 70 (Fra Luca Bartolomeo de Pacioli (c. 1447 – 1517)).

1518 – Leonardo was 66 when his pupil for 28 years Gian Giacomo Caprotti da Oreno, better known as Salaì (1480 – 19 Jan 1524, aged 44), Italian artist and pupil of Leonardo da Vinci for 28 years, from 1490 (age 10) to 1518 (age 38); he painted under the name Andrea Salai), left.

1519 – 2 May - Leonardo died of stroke at Clos Lucé, in Amboise, France, aged 67 years and 17 days. He is remembered as an Italian polymath whose areas of interest included invention, painting, sculpting, architecture, science, music, mathematics, engineering, literature, anatomy, geology, astronomy, optics, botany, hydrodynamics, writing, history, and cartography, but he did not publish his findings. He is the father of paleontology, ichnology, and architecture, and is one of the greatest painters of all time.

Michelangelo was 44 years 1 month and 27 days when Leonardo died.

Leonardo da Vinci was buried in the Chapel of Saint-Hubert in Château d'Amboise, in the Loire Valley, in France, 200 km southwest of Paris, 900 km northwest of Florence. Following the chapel's destruction in 1802, the whereabouts of Leonardo's remains became subject to dispute. While excavating the site in 1863, the poet Arsène Houssaye found a partially-complete skeleton, and stone fragments bearing the inscription 'EO [...] DUS VINC'. The unusually large skull led Houssaye to conclude he had located the remains of Leonardo, which were re-interred in their present location of the chapel of Saint-Hubert, also at the Chateau d'Amboise. A plaque above the tomb states that the remains are only "presumed" to be those of Leonardo. In 2016, it was announced that DNA tests were to be conducted to investigate the veracity of the attribution, with results expected in 2019.

Maybe 15 of his paintings have survived, 1 wax sculpture, and over 13,000 pages of notes and drawings. These notebooks have found their way into major collections, such as the Royal Library at Windsor Castle, the Louvre, the Biblioteca Nacional de España, the

Victoria and Albert Museum, the Biblioteca Ambrosiana in Milan, which holds the twelve-volume Codex Atlanticus, and British Library in London, which has put a selection from the Codex Arundel online. The Codex Leicester is the only major scientific work of Leonardo in private hands; it is owned by Bill Gates, and is displayed once a year in different cities around the world.

1520 – Michelangelo, 45, designed and carved tombs for the Medici family and Medici Chapel, for 14 years, until 1534.

The Medici came back to Michelangelo with another grand proposal, this time for a family funerary chapel in the Basilica of San Lorenzo. Michelangelo used his own discretion to create the composition of the Medici Chapel, which houses the large tombs of two of the younger members of the Medici family, Giuliano, Duke of Nemours, and Lorenzo, his nephew. It also serves to commemorate their more famous predecessors, Lorenzo the Magnificent and his brother Giuliano, who are buried nearby. The tombs display statues of the two Medici and allegorical figures representing Night and Day, and Dusk and Dawn. The chapel also contains Michelangelo's Medici Madonna. In 1976 a concealed corridor was discovered with drawings on the walls that related to the chapel itself.

The work to reconstruct the façade of the Basilica of San Lorenzo in Florence, and to adorn it with sculptures, which started 7 years ago, in 1513, was abruptly cancelled by Michelangelo's financially strapped patrons, before any real progress had been made. The basilica lacks a façade to this day.

1521 – 1 December – Michelangelo was 46.7 when Pope Leo X died (11 Dec 1475 – 1 Dec 1521, aged 45.9, Pope for 8.6 years: 9 March 1513 – 1 Dec 1521)

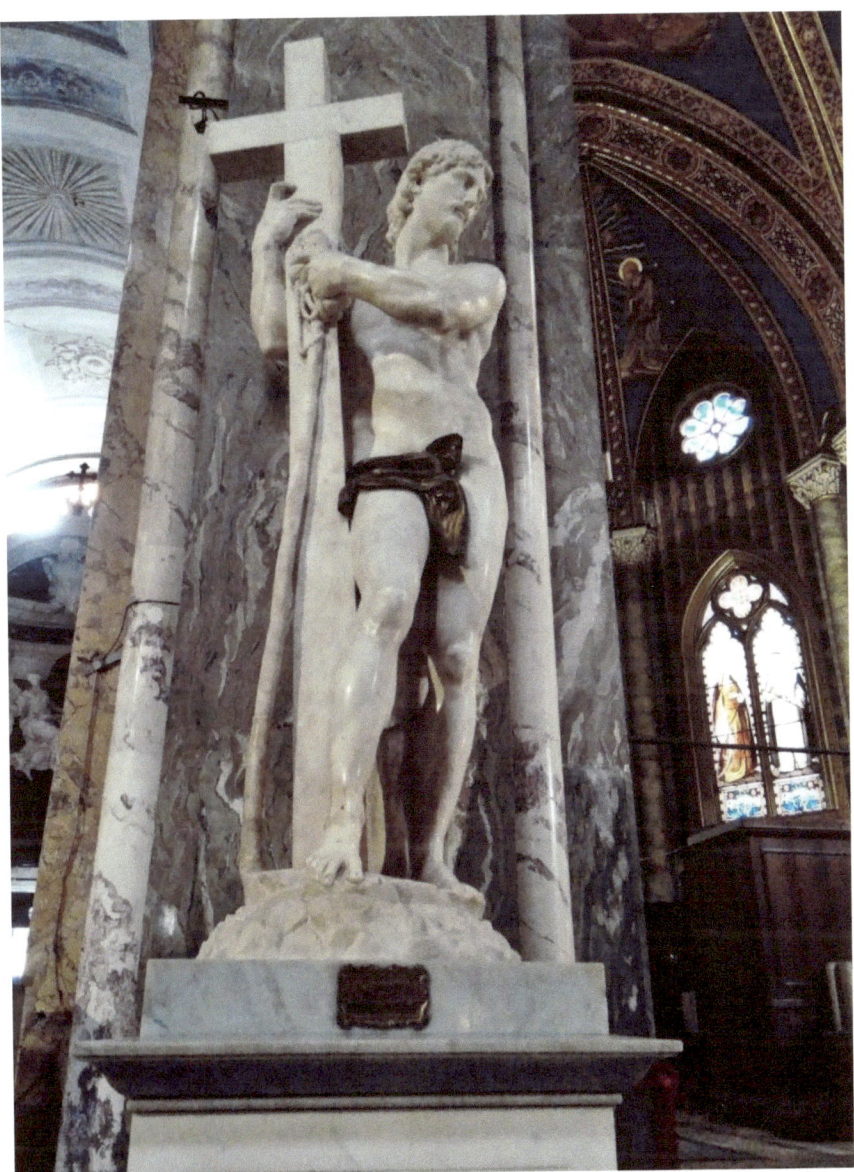

Italy, Rome (753 BC, one of the oldest continuously occupied cities in Europe, called Roma Aeterna (The Eternal City) and Caput Mundi (Capital of the World)), the marble sculpture Cristo della Minerva by Michelangelo Buonarotti (1475 – 1564, sculptor, painter, architect, poet and engineer, the greatest artist of all time), finished in 1521, located to the left of the main altar in Basilica di Santa Maria sopra Minerva (1280-1370, 101 m by 41 m).

1522 – 9 January - Michelangelo was 46.8 when a new Pope was elected: Pope Adrian VI, 62.8, (2 March 1459 – 14 Sep 1523, aged 64.5, Papacy for 1.7 years: 9 Jan 1522 – 14 Sep 1523, the only Dutchman to become pope, he was the last non-Italian pope until John Paul II, 455 years later, in 1976).

1523 – Death of Pietro Perugino (1446 – 1523, aged 77, Italian painter), 6 years older than Leonardo, but died 4 years after him.

14 September - Michelangelo was 48.5 when Pope Adrian VI died (2 March 1459 – 14 Sep 1523, aged 64.5, Papacy for 1.7 years: 9 Jan 1522 – 14 Sep 1523).

16 October – Death in Cortona (80 km southeast of Florence, 160 km north of Rome, elevation 500 m) of Luca Signorelli (c. 1450, Cortona — 16 October 1523, Cortona, aged 73), Italian painter, born Luca d'Egidio di Ventura in Cortona, Tuscany (some sources call him Luca da Cortona). Luca Signorelli was 2 years older than Leonardo, and died 4 years after him.

19 November – election of Pope Clement VII, 45.5, (26 May 1478 – 25 Sep 1534, aged 56.3, Papacy for 10.8 years: 19 Nov 1523 – 25 Sep 1534, born Giulio di Giuliano de' Medici, cousin of Pope Leo X).

1524 – Michelangelo, 49, was commissioned by Pope Clement VII, 46, to design the Laurentian Library at San Lorenzo's Church. He designed both the interior of the library itself and its vestibule. It was left to assistants to interpret his plans and carry out instructions. The library was not opened for 47 years, until 1571, and the vestibule remained incomplete for 380 years, until 1904.

1527 – 6 May – Michelangelo was 52.1 when took place the occupation of Rome (then part of the Papal States) by the mutinous troops (14,000 Germans and 6,000 Spanish) of Charles V, Holy Roman Emperor. It was an imperial victory in the conflict between Charles and the League of Cognac (1526–1529) — the alliance of France, Milan, Venice, Florence and the Papacy. Emperor Charles V was greatly embarrassed by the fact that he had been powerless to stop his troops striking against Pope Clement VII, 49, and imprisoning him. It is considered the beginning of the decline, after about 200 years, of the Italian Renaissance, which influenced all Europe, including Russia, in many ways.

Florentine citizens, encouraged by the attack on Rome, threw out the Medici, and restored the republic. A siege of the city ensued, and Michelangelo went to the aid of his Florence.

21 June - Niccolò di Bernardo dei Machiavelli died (3 May 1469 – 21 June 1527, aged 58.1), Italian diplomat, politician, historian, philosopher, humanist, writer, playwright and poet.

1528 – Michelangelo, 53, worked on Florence's fortifications from this year to the next.

2 July - Michelangelo was 53.3 when his second brother Buonarroto Buonarroti Simoni died (1477 – 2 July 1528, aged 51). He was married twice, and had two sons and a daughter.

1530 – Michelangelo was 55 when Florence fell, and the Medici were restored to power, but Michelangelo fell out of favor.

He carved Bound slave, known as Atlas, for Pope Julius' tomb.

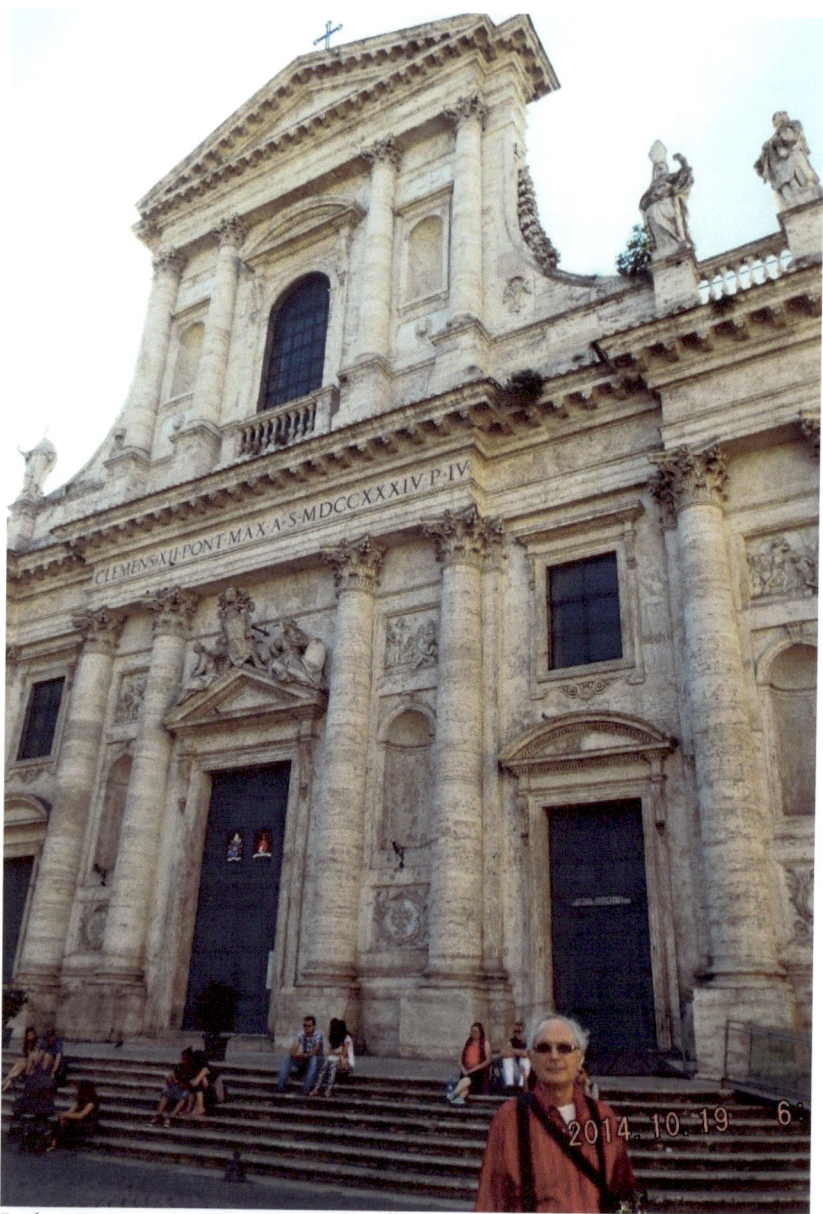

Italy, Roma, in Piazza dell Oro, on Via Acciaioli and near Via Giulia, in rione Ponte, Chiesa San Giovanni dei Fiorentini (1523-1734), architects include Michelangelo (1475–1564), Carlo Maderno (1556–1629), Francesco Borromini (1599–1667), inscription: CLEMENS XII PONT MAX A S MDCCXXXIV P IV.

1532 – 1 May – Michelangelo was 57.1 when the young Alessandro de' Medici, 21.7, (22 July 1510 – 6 Jan 1537, aged 26.5, Duke of Florence for 4.6 years: 1 May 1532 – 6 Jan 1537), had been installed as the first Duke of Florence. Michelangelo fled to Rome, leaving assistants to complete the Medici chapel and the Laurentian Library. Despite Michelangelo's support of the republic, he was welcomed by Pope Clement VII, 54, who reinstated an allowance that he had previously granted the artist, and made a new contract with him for a smaller tomb of Pope Julius II, who died 19 years ago.

1534 – Michelangelo was 59 when his father Ludovico di Leonardo di Buonarroti Simoni died at the age of 90 (1444 – 1534).

Shortly before his death on 25 Sep, Pope Clement VII commissioned Michelangelo to paint a fresco of The Last Judgement on the altar wall of the Sistine Chapel (Capella Sistina, a chapel in the Apostolic Palace, the official residence of the Pope, in Vatican City, started 1473, completed 1481, consecrated 15 August 1483, height 20.7 m. Originally known as the Cappella Magna, the chapel takes its name from Pope Sixtus IV (21 July 1414 – 12 August 1484, aged 70 years and 22 days, Pope for 13 years and 3 days: 9 Aug 1471 – 12 Aug 1484), who restored it between 1477 and 1480.

25 September - Pope Clement VII died at age 56.3, (26 May 1478 – 25 Sep 1534, Papacy for 10.8 years: 19 Nov 1523 – 25 Sep 1534, born Giulio di Giuliano de' Medici, cousin of Pope Leo X).

13 October – Cardinal Alessandro Farnese, 66.6, became Pope Paul III (29 Feb 1468 – 10 Nov 1549, aged 81.8, Pope for 15 years and 28 days: 13 Oct 1534 – 10 Nov 1549)

Pope Paul III, was involved in seeing that Michelangelo began and completed the fresco of The Last Judgement, which he labored on from 1534 to October 1541. Pope Paul III insisted the artist undertake the Last Judgement, which took him 7 years to paint.

Michelangelo also finished the Statue of Victory, which is now in Palazzo Vecchio in Firenze.

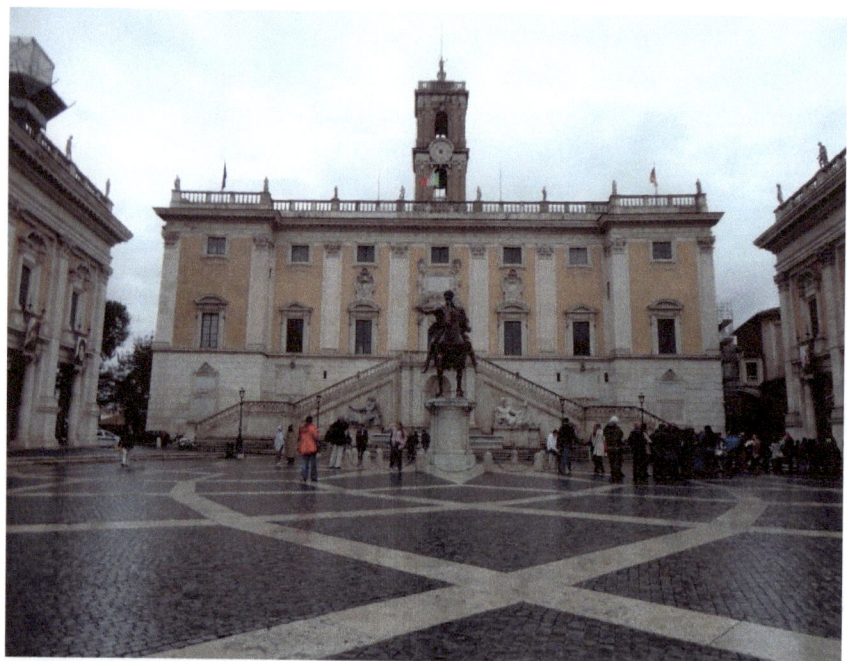

Piazza del Campidoglio has three main Palazzi. Palazzo Senatorio (back, now Rome's city hall), built around 1250-1350 atop the Tabularium (78 BC, housed the archives of the ancient Rome), re-used blocks from the Tabularium, and was modified by Michelangelo around 1535. The Palazzo dei Conservatori (right) was built around 1550, for the local magistrate, on top of a temple (about 550 BC) dedicated to Jupiter "Maximus Capitolinus". Michelangelo's renovation of it incorporated many new architectural ideas. Palazzo Nuovo (left) was built around 1650, based on Michelangelo's ideas, with an identical exterior design to the Palazzo dei Conservatori, which it faces across the piazza. The Capitoline Museums are inside all these three Palazzi surrounding the Piazza del Campidoglio, and interlinked by an underground gallery beneath the piazza. Until around 1475, the main market of the city of Rome was held on and around the Piazza del Campidoglio, while cattle continued to be taxed and sold in the ancient forum located just to the south. Michelangelo Buonarroti (1475 – 1564) had a key role in the design and updating of the Piazza del Campidoglio and its surrounding Palazzi.

1536 – Michelangelo, 61, in Rome was painting for two years the Last Judgement in the Sistine Chapel, which was completed and unveiled after 5 years, in October 1541.

He was also commissioned by the Farnese Pope Paul III, 68, to design the Piazza del Campidoglio and the surrounding palazzi, because the Pope wanted a symbol of the new Rome to impress Charles V, 36, (24 Feb 1500 – 21 Sep 1558, aged 58.6, Holy Roman Emperor (including Romans, Italy, Spain, Germany, Burgundy, Netherlands, and Austria: 28 June 1519 – 27 August 1556), who was expected in 1538. Michelangelo's first designs for the piazza and remodeling of the surrounding palazzi date from this year, 1536. His plan was very extensive, including its trapezoid piazza displaying the ancient bronze statue of Marcus Aurelius. Executing the design was slow: Little was actually completed in Michelangelo's lifetime, but work continued loyally to his designs, and the Campidoglio was completed after more than 120 years, in the 17th century, except for the paving design, which was to be finished over 300 years later.

In Rome, Michelangelo lived near Trajan's column (113 AD) and the church of Santa Maria di Loreto (construction of this church began 25 years earlier, in 1507, by Antonio da Sangallo the younger, and will be finished after 50 years, in 1582). It was at this time that he met the poet Vittoria Colonna, 44, Marchesa di Pescara (April 1492 – 25 Feb 1547, aged 54.8, wife (for 16 years: 1509 – 1525, form age 17 to 33) of Fernando Francesco d'Avalos (1489 – 3 Dec 1525, aged 36), Marquis of Pescara, widow at 33, Italian noblewoman and poet), who was to become one of his closest friends until her death in 1547.

At the age of 44, Vittoria was back in Rome, where, besides winning the esteem of Cardinals Reginald Pole and Contarini, she became the object of a passionate friendship on the part of 61-year-old Michelangelo. The great artist addressed some of his finest sonnets to her, made drawings for her, and spent long hours in her company. She created a gift manuscript of spiritual poetry for him.

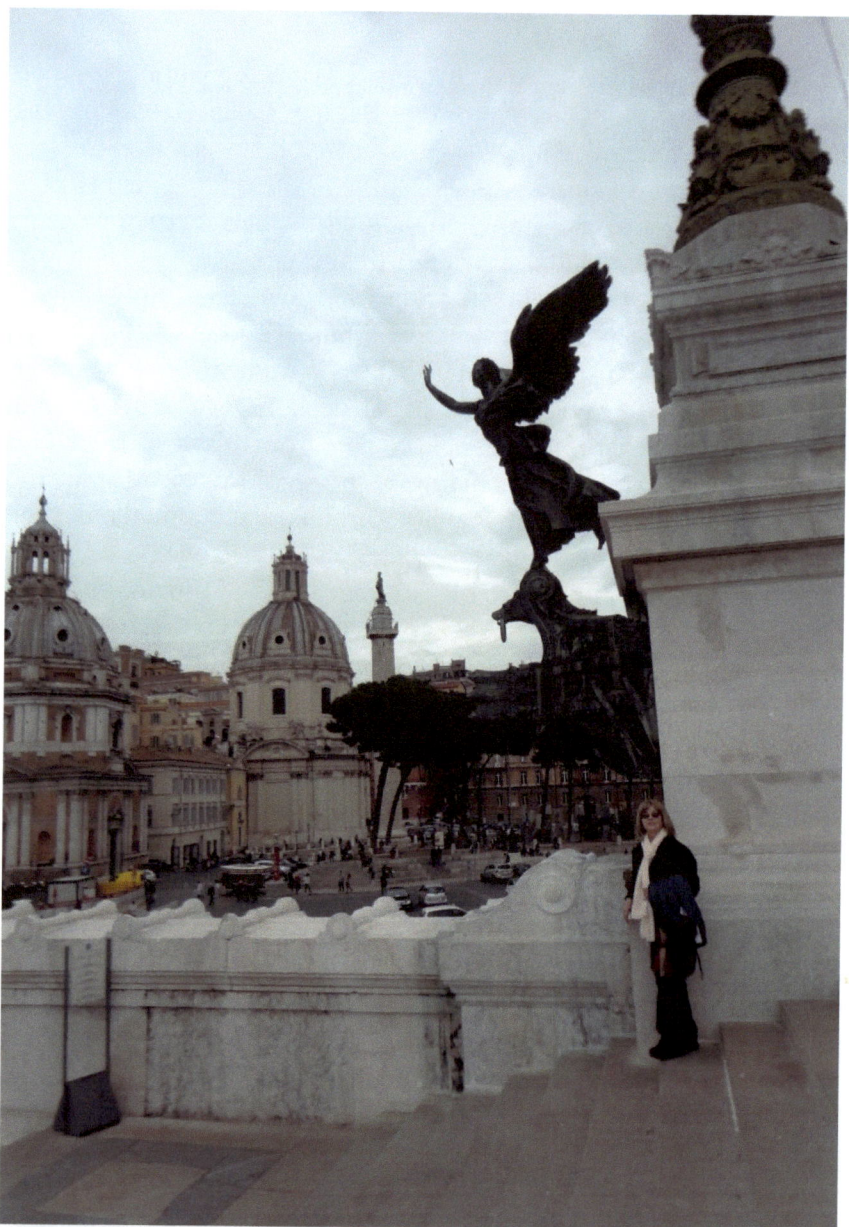

Italia, Roma: Detail of the north-east side of the Monumento Nazionale a Vittorio Emanuele II, or Altare della Patria, or "Il Vittoriano" (1925, right), Trajan's column (113 AD, center), and the churches Santissimo Nome di Maria al Foro Traiano (1751, center-left), and Santa Maria di Loreto (1582, left).

1537 – 12 January - Death of Lorenzo di Credi (1459 – 12 Jan 1537, aged 78), Italian painter.

Francisco de Holanda, 20, (6 Sep 1517 – 19 June 1585, aged 67.7, Portuguese painter, architect and sculptor) painted Michelangelo, 62, drawn from the left sight.

1540 – Michelangelo, 65, finished The Pietà of Vittoria Colonna, 48, a chalk drawing of a type described as "presentation drawings", as they might be given as a gift by an artist.

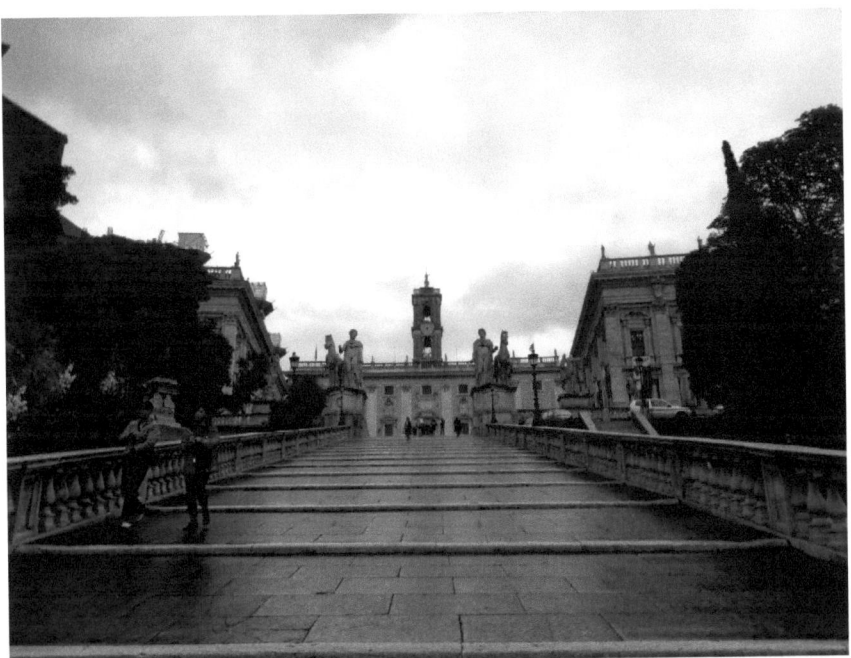

The steps (cordonata) to the Piazza del Campidoglio, which was built around 1050 and updated by Michelangelo around 1535.

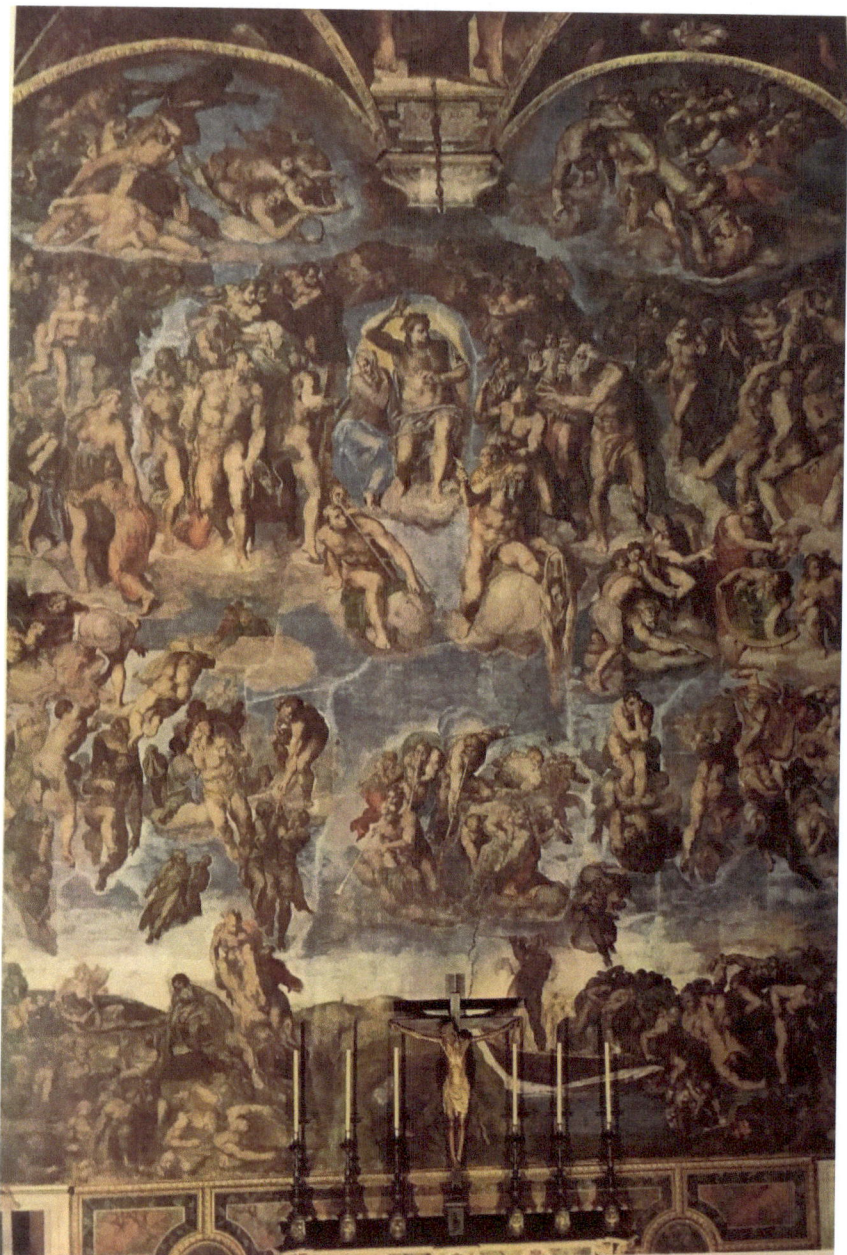

1541 – October - Michelangelo, 66.6, finished painting the Last Judgement (1536-1541), on the altar wall in the Sistine Chapel.

The work covers the entire altar wall, and consists of 314 figures in tumultuous motion, depicting the Second Coming of Christ and his Judgement of the souls. All figures, young and old, are athletic nudes. Above, in lunettes on either side, are throngs of angels carrying the instruments of Christ's Passion: on the left, the Cross, and on the right, the pillar where he was scourged. The middle area represents the kingdom of Heaven. Christ, a massive, muscular figure, youthful, beardless and naked, in a classic pose, raises his right hand in judgement. On his left are the Apostles, and on His right, the Patriarchs. Angels sound their trumpets, while the resurrected bodies at the lower left rise from their graves, and ascend towards Heaven. The figures at the center right fall, condemned, to suffer in Hell.

The depiction of Christ and the Virgin Mary naked was considered sacrilegious, and Cardinal Carafa and Monsignor Sernini (Mantua's ambassador) campaigned to have the fresco removed or censored, but the Pope resisted. At the Council of Trent, shortly before Michelangelo's death in 1564, it was decided to obscure the genitals and Daniele da Volterra, an apprentice of Michelangelo, was commissioned to make the alterations. An uncensored copy of the original, by Marcello Venusti, is in the Capodimonte Museum of Naples.

Michelangelo also designed the upper floor of the Palazzo Farnese, and the interior of the Church of Santa Maria degli Angeli, in which he transformed the vaulted interior of an Ancient Roman bathhouse. Other architectural works include San Giovanni dei Fiorentini, the Sforza Chapel (Capella Sforza) in the Basilica di Santa Maria Maggiore, and the Porta Pia.

Vittoria Colonna, 49, had to move to Orvieto and Viterbo, on the occasion of her brother Ascanio Colonna's revolt against Pope Paul III, but this produced no change in her relations with Michelangelo, 66, and they continued to visit and correspond as before.

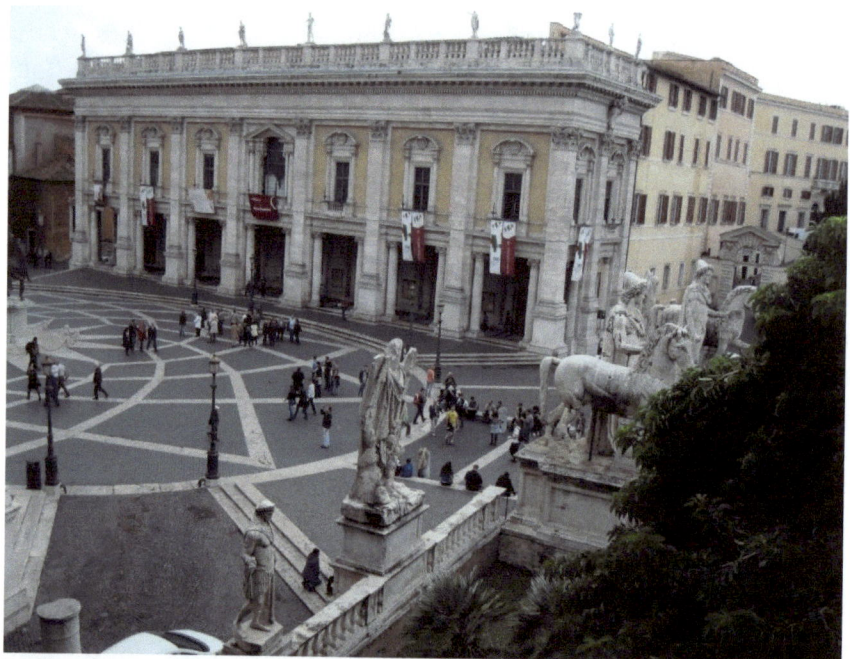

Italia, Roma, Palazzo dei Conservatori (circa 1450, built on a Jupiter temple Maximus Capitolinus, from 550 BC), in Piazza del Campidoglio built by Michelangelo.

<u>**1542**</u> – Michelangelo, 67, received another commission for the Vatican. This was for the painting of two large frescos in the Cappella Paolina, depicting significant events in the lives of the two most important saints of Rome: The Conversion of Saint Paul and The Crucifixion of Saint Peter. Like the Last Judgement, these two works are complex compositions containing a great number of figures, and they were completed after 8 years, in 1550.

Also, he made a drawing of Vittoria Colonna, 50.

<u>**1543**</u> – Vesalius published Leonardo's work on anatomy and physiology in "De humani corporis fabrica". Leonardo was the first to define atherosclerosis and liver cirrhosis. He created models of the cerebral ventricles with the use of melted wax, and constructed a glass aorta to observe the circulation of blood through the aortic valve, by using water and grass seed to watch flow patterns.

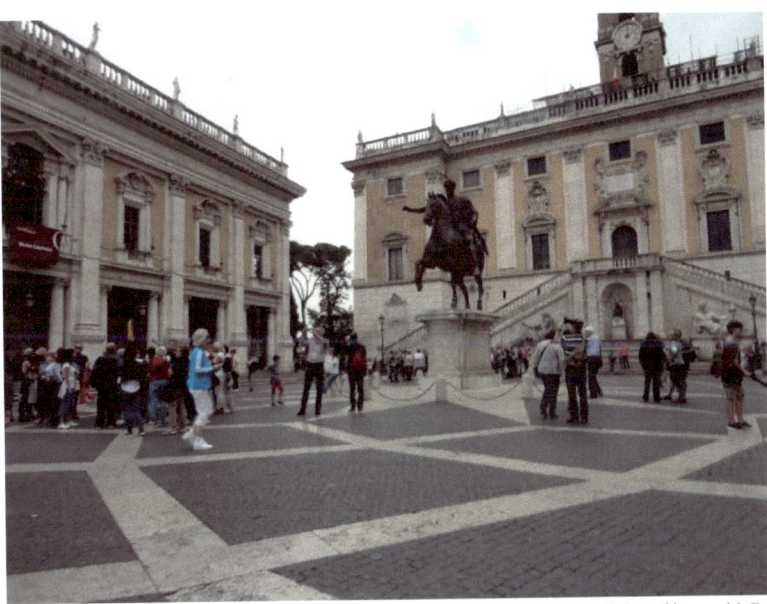

Italy, Rome (753 BC), Piazza del Campidoglio (1546 by Michelangelo, paving completed in 1940, on Collis Capitolinus, the oldest part of Rome, with Temple of Jupiter (509 BC)), a replica of the equestrian bronze statue (175, the oldest, moved here in 1538) of Marcus Aurelius (born 121, Emperor 161-180), Palazzo Senatorio (right, 1350, bell-tower 1582, atop Tabularium, now the city hall), Palazzo Nuovo (left, 1603-1654, opened 1734).

1545 – Michelangelo, 70, had the Tomb of Julius II completed and installed in San Pietro in Vincoli, Rome. He was still working on the Pauline Chapel frescoes, for 5 more years, to 1550.

1546 – Michelangelo, 71, was appointed chief architect at St. Peter's Basilica in Rome, and of the Farnese Palace.

The process of replacing the 1200 years old Constantinian basilica of the 4th century had been underway for fifty years, and in 1506 foundations had been laid to the plans of Bramante. Successive architects had worked on it, but little progress had been made. Michelangelo was persuaded to take over the project. He returned to the concepts of Bramante, and developed his ideas for a centrally planned church, strengthening the structure both physically and visually. The dome was not completed until after his death.

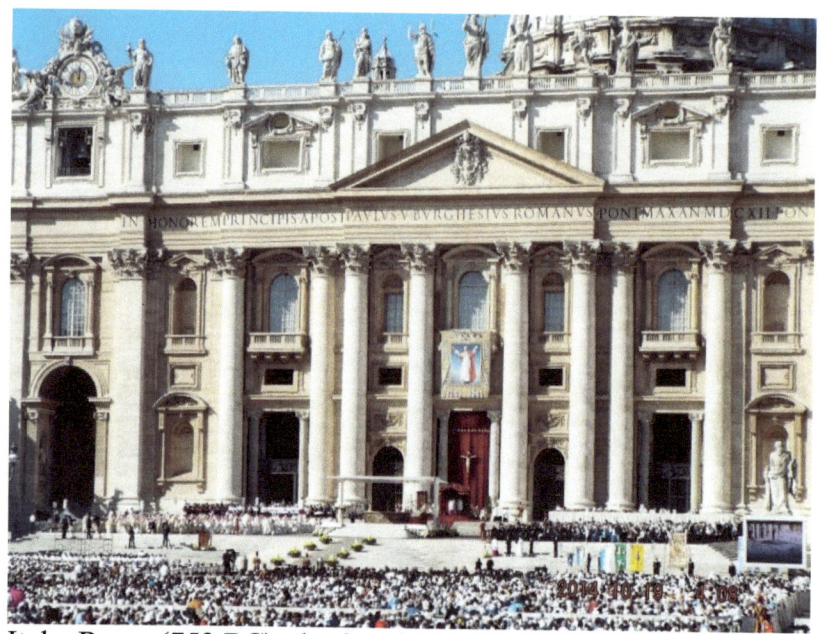

Italy, Rome (753 BC), the façade (114 m by 47 m, Maderno) of Basilica Sancti Petri (1506–1626, 132 m), a mass with the Pope.

1547 – 25 February – Michelangelo was 71.9 when his close friend the poet Vittoria Colonna, Marchesa di Pescara died at age 54.8 (April 1492 – 25 Feb 1547, wife (for 16 years: 1509 – 1525, form age 17 to 33) of Fernando Francesco d'Avalos (1489 – 3 Dec 1525, aged 36), Marquis of Pescara, widow at 33, Italian noblewoman and poet),

31 March – Death of the King of France Francis I at 52.5, (12 Sep 1494 – 31 March 1547, King for 32 years and 3 months: 1 Jan 1515 – 31 March 1547).

1548 – 9 January - Michelangelo was 72.8 when his third brother Giovan Simone Buonarroti Simoni died (11 March 1479 – 9 Jan 1548, aged 68.8). He was married and had a son.

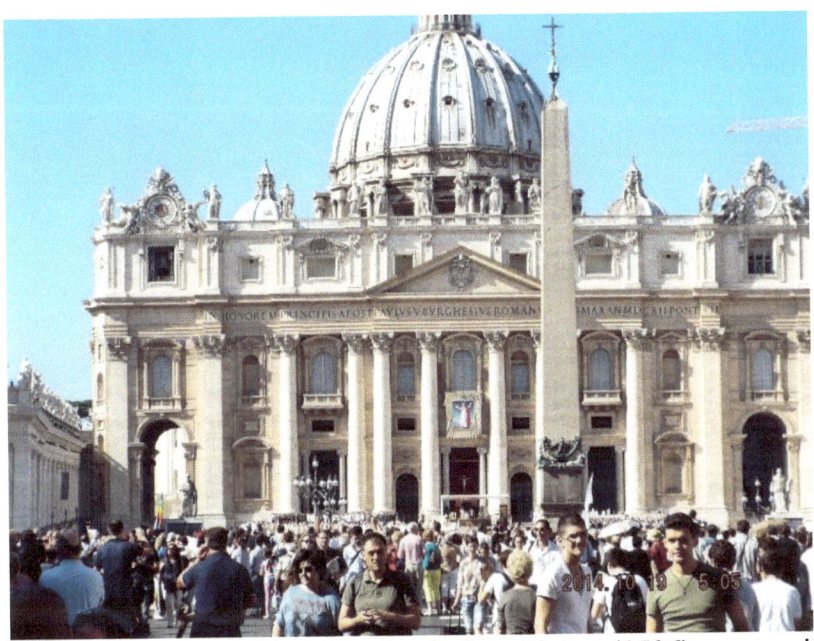

Italy, Vatican, Basilica Papale di San Pietro (1506), an ancient Egyptian obelisk (center right, of red granite, 25.5 m, 41 m total, from Heliopolis, Egypt, 2400 BC, moved by Emperor Augustus in 30 BC to Alexandria, in 37 to Rome, here in 1586).

1550 – Michelangelo was 75 when Giorgio Vasari's "*Le Vite de' più eccellenti pittori, scultori, e architettori* (Lives of the most excellent Painters, Sculptors and Architects)" was published, and features Michelangelo.

The Conversion of Saint Paul and The Crucifixion of Saint Peter, with a great number of figures, were completed by Michelangelo, after 8 years of work.

1553 – Michelangelo was 78 when Ascanio Condivi's "Life of Michelangelo" was published.

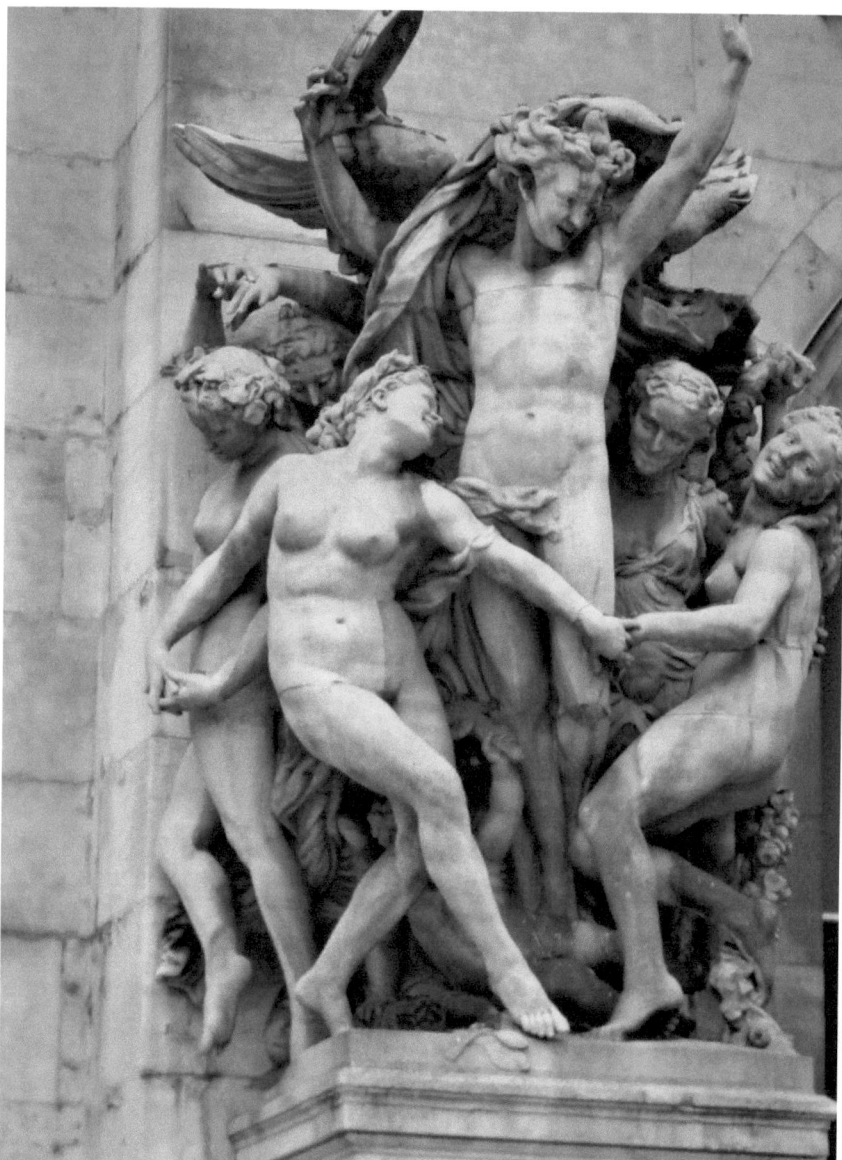

Paris - A copy (made in 1964) of the sculpture "The Dance" (1868 – 1869, 4.2 m by 3 m, with a highly animated central male dancer, surrounded by six dancing women (the original is now in the Musée d'Orsay)) by Jean-Baptiste Carpeaux (1827 – 1875, he closely studied the sculpture of Michelangelo (1475 – 1564) in Rome; Garnier commissioned Carpeaux in 1865), on the left side of the right outer bay on the façade of l'Opéra de Paris (1875).

1555 – Michelangelo, 80, completed the Florentine Pietà, in which he depicts himself, this time as the aged Nicodemus lowering the body of Jesus from the cross into the arms of Mary his mother, and Mary Magdalene.

13 November - Michelangelo was 80.6 when his fourth brother Sigismondo Buonarroti Simoni died (22 Jan 1481 – 13 Nov 1555, aged 74.8).

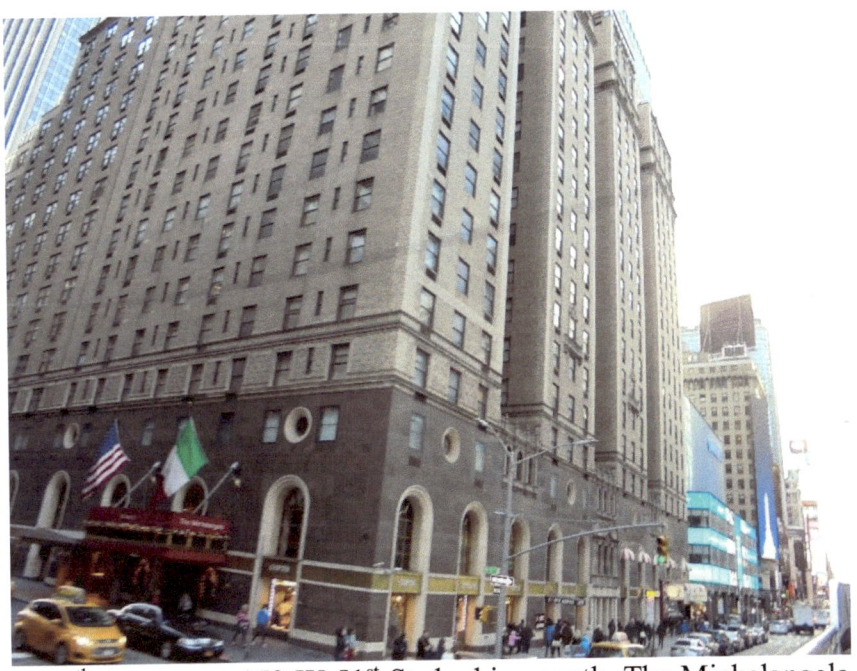

On 7th Avenue at 152 W 51st St, looking south, The Michelangelo Hotel (1926, in the former Taft Hotel building, 22 stories, 178 rooms, 69 m).

1560 – Michelangelo, 85, completed wooden model of St. Peter's dome.

1563 – 6 March - Michelangelo was 88 when a portrait of Michelangelo on a medal, for his 88th birthday, was produced by Leone Leoni, 54, (1509 – 22 July 1590, aged 81, Italian sculptor and medalist)

1564 – Michelangelo, 88.8, worked on the Rondanini Pietà from 1552 until six days before his death, it is now in Milan.

18 February - Michelangelo died at 88 years 11 months and 12 days, at home in Macel de'Corvi, Rome.

His tomb in the Basilica of Santa Croce, Florence.

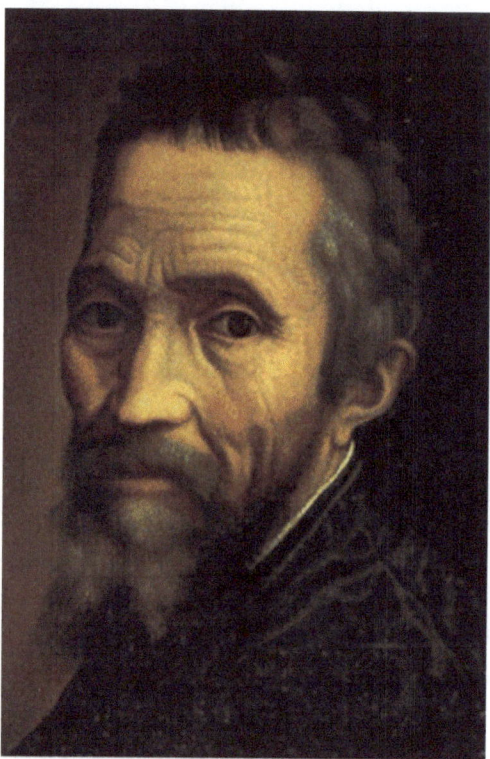

Michelangelo

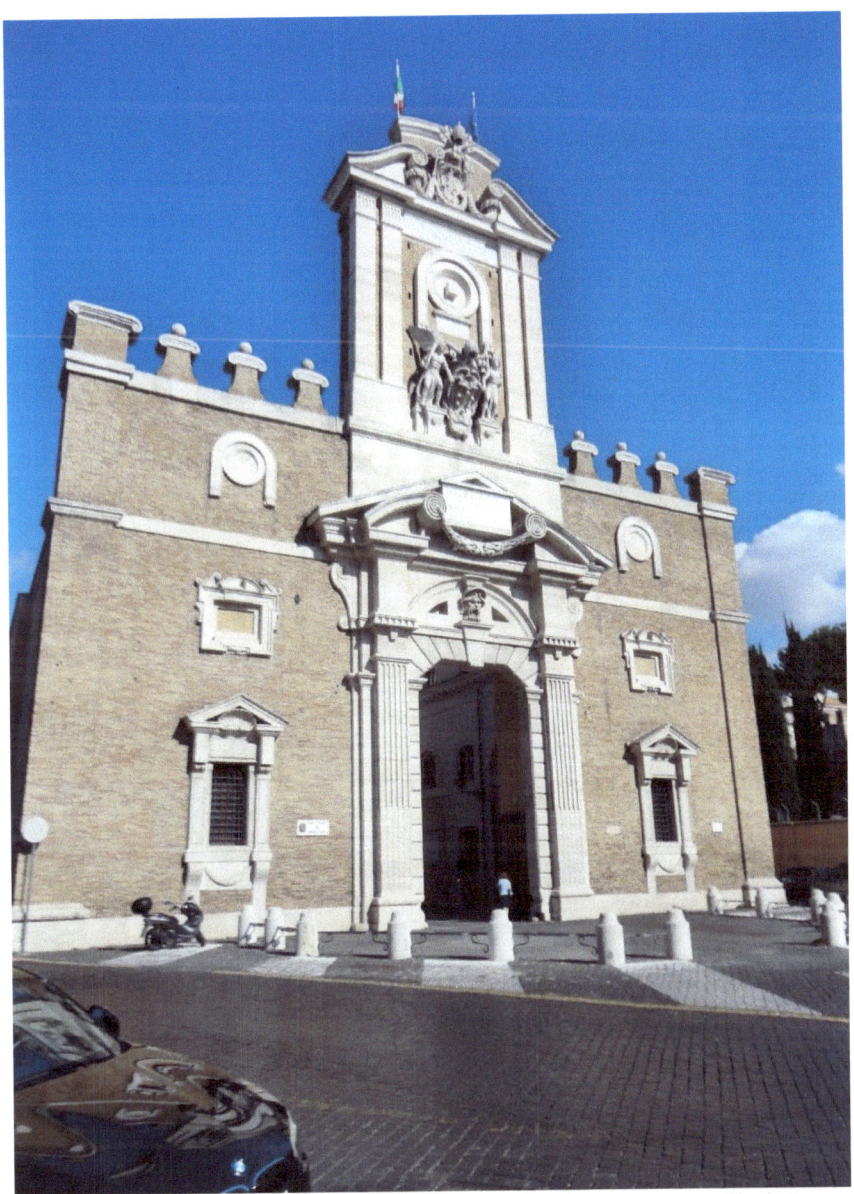

Italy, Rome (753 BC, one of the oldest cities in Europe, called Roma Aeterna (The Eternal City) and Caput Mundi (Capital of the World)), the southwest of the internal façade of Porta Pia (1561 - 1565, by Pope Pius IV (1499-1565), designed by Michelangelo (1475-1564, his last architectural work), a gate in the Aurelian (214-275) Walls (275) of Rome, to replace Porta Nomentana (273)), with the Museo Storico dei Bersaglieri (sharpshooters).

1574 – 27 June – Death of Giorgio Vasari (30 July 1511 – 27 June 1574, aged 62.9), Italian painter, architect, writer, and historian, most famous today for his "Lives of the Most Excellent Painters, Sculptors, and Architects", considered the foundation of art-historical writing.

1577 – 28 June – Birth of Sir Peter Paul Rubens (28 June 1577 – 30 May 1640, aged 62.9, great Flemish painter, father of eight children (3 with his first wife Isabella, and 5 with his second wife Helena)).

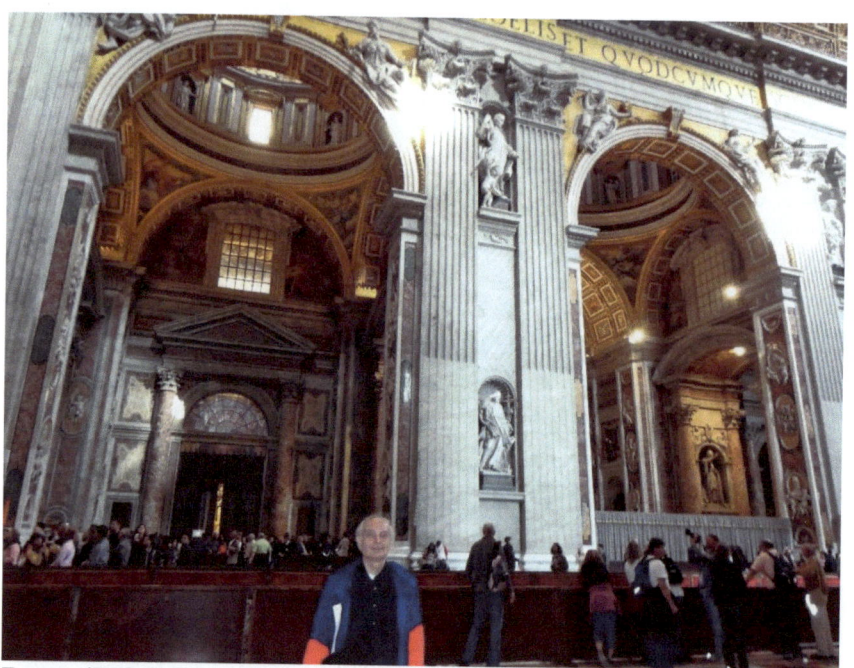

Rome (753 BC), Vatican City State (1929): part of the northern side of the nave of the Basilica di San Pietro (1506 – 1626,), designed by Michelangelo and finished by Maderno,

Chapter 3. Rembrandt

1589 – 8 October - Rembrandt's parents, both 21 years old, marry in the reformed Pieterskerk in Leiden.

Rembrandt's father, Harmen Gerritszoon van Rijn, 21, (1568 – 27 April 1630, aged 62, the river Rijn) was a miller and the only member of his family who converted from Roman Catholicism to Protestantism (he belonged to the Dutch Reformed Church).

Rembrandt's mother, Neeltgen Willemsdochter van Zuijtbrouck, 21, (1568 – 1640, aged 72), was the daughter of a baker, Willem Adriaensz Zuijtbroeck (c 1533 – 14 June 1609, aged c 76) and his wife Lijsbeth Cornelisdr (1535 – 1603, aged 68), all Roman Catholics.

Rembrandt's parents had 10 children: son Gerrit Harmenszoon van Rijn (1590 – 20 Sep 1631, aged 41), daughter Machtelt (circa 1592 – 6 Sep 1625, aged 33), son Cornelis (c 1594 – c 1639, aged c 43), son Adriaan (1597 – 1652, aged 55), son Willem (c 1599 – 26 August 1655, aged c 56), Rembrandt (15 July 1606 – 4 Oct 1669, aged 63), daughter Lysbeth van Rijn (circa 1608 – 28 Oct 1655, aged c 47).

Two died in infancy and one has no records. Rembrandt was the 9th child.

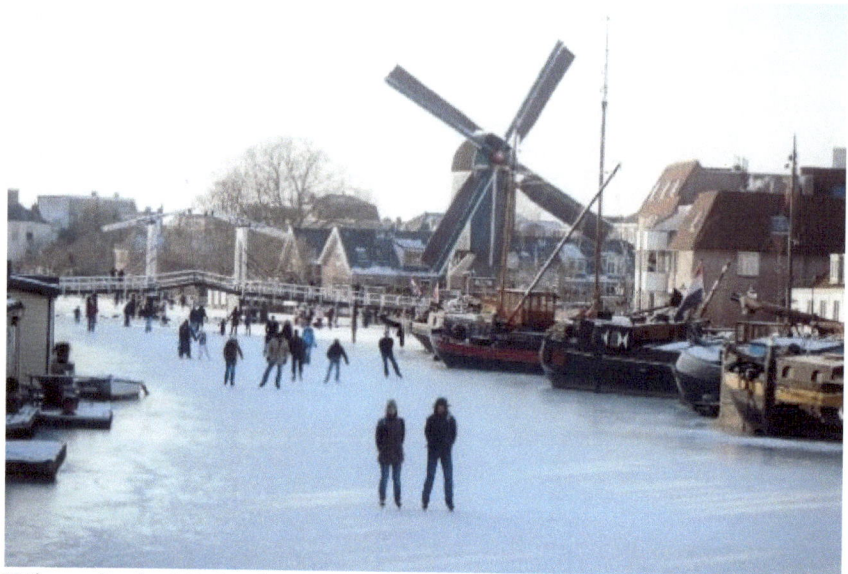
Winter in the Netherlands

1606 – 15 July – Rembrandt Harmenszoon van Rijn was born in Leiden (elevation 0 m, 35 km southwest of Amsterdam, and 15 km northeast of The Hague), Dutch Republic (now the Netherlands) – both parents were 38 years old.

His older brother Adriaan Harmenszoon van Rijn was 9 years old (1597 – 1652, aged 55).

Rubens was 29 years and 17 days.

1609 – 14 June – Rembrandt was 2.9 years old when his grandfather, from the mother side, Willem Adriaensz Zuijtbroeck, passed away at circa 76 (c 1533 – 14 June 1609).

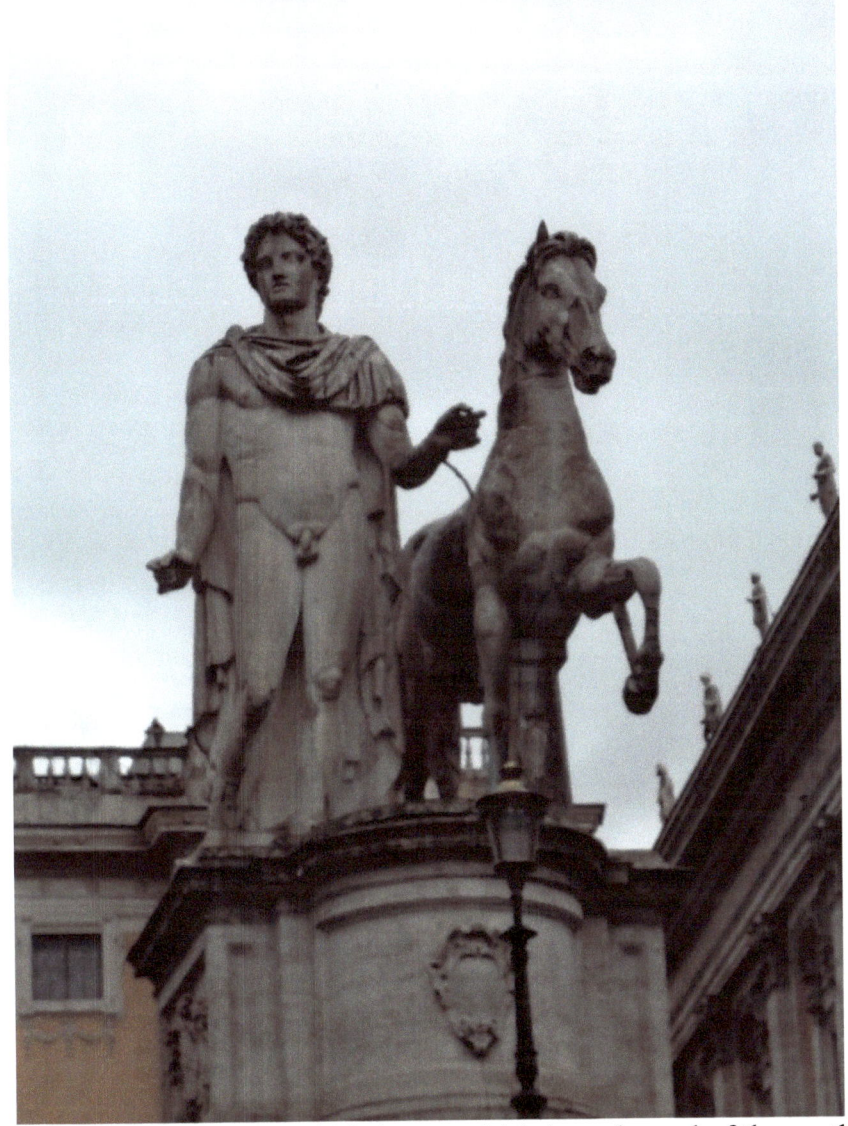

The statue of Pollux and his horse, which is at the end of the south railings of Michelangelo's epic and wide-ramped stair (the cordonata), that is gradually ascending the hill to reach the high Piazza del Campidoglio. Palazzo Senatorio (back left, now Rome's city hall), built around 1250-1350 atop the Tabularium (78 BC, housed the archives of the ancient Rome), and was modified by Michelangelo around 1535. Palazzo dei Conservatori (1550, right back) was also redesigned by Michelangelo (1475 – 1564).

1613 – Rembrandt van Rijn, 7, starts attending the Latin School, to prepare for admission to Leiden University. The school trained their students in grammar and rhetoric, and lessons were based on classical literature. Rembrandt received a thorough grounding in classical and biblical stories.

1617 – 2 February – Rembrandt was 10.6 when his older brother Adriaan, 20, married Lijsbeth Simons van Leeuwen; they had a daughter Cornelia Ariens van Rijn born in 1629, when Adriaan was 32.

1619 – Rembrandt, 13, was apprenticed by his father, who observed his son's painting talents, to Jacob Isaacszoon van Swanenburgh, 48, (1571 – 1638, aged 67). Van Swanenburgh was a Roman Catholic, his father was burgomaster 5 times, and held other major town offices. Rembrandt studied with him for about 3 years, until 1622. Van Swanenburgh painted in Venice, Rome and Naples for 17 years: 1600 - 1617. He married a Neapolitan woman.

1620 – 16 May - Rembrandt, 13.8 (2 months before his 14th birthday), was enrolled by his father at the University of Leiden (1575) where he studied history, rhetorical gestures, historical veracity, textual accuracy.

1622 – 1 October – Rembrandt, 16.2, finished studies with van Swanenburgh, and was living with his parents in Leiden's Weddesteeg, together with his 2 older brothers and one sister Gerrit, Machtelt, Cornelis, and with the younger sister Lysbeth. His older brothers Willem and Adriaen have left home.

1624 – Rembrandt, 18, had a brief but important apprenticeship of six months with the painter Pieter Lastman, 41, (1583 – 1633, aged 50) in Amsterdam, and also studied painting with painter Jacob Pynas, 32, (1592 – 1650, aged 58). Many of his contemporaries traveled to Italy, as part of their artistic training, but Rembrandt never left the Dutch Republic during his lifetime.

He painted The Spectacles-pedlar, The Three Singers, The Operation, The Unconscious Patient.

1625 – Rembrandt, 18.5, with the help of his father, sets up a studio as an independent painter in Leiden, living at home with his parents. He shared his studio, for about 6 years, until 1631, with his younger friend and colleague Jan Lievens, 17.3, (24 Oct 1607 – 4 June 1674, aged 66.6).

The Stoning of Stephen is Rembrandt's earliest dated painting.

6 September – Rembrandt was 19.1, when his older sister Machtelt passed away at circa 33 (circa 1592 – 6 Sep 1625).

1626 – Rembrandt, 20, painted Christ Driving the Moneychangers from the Temple, Bust of a Man Wearing a Gorget and Plumed Beret, History Painting, David with the Head of Goliath before Saul, The Baptism of the Eunuch, Balaam and the Ass, Musical Allegory, Tobit Accusing Anna of Stealing the Kid.

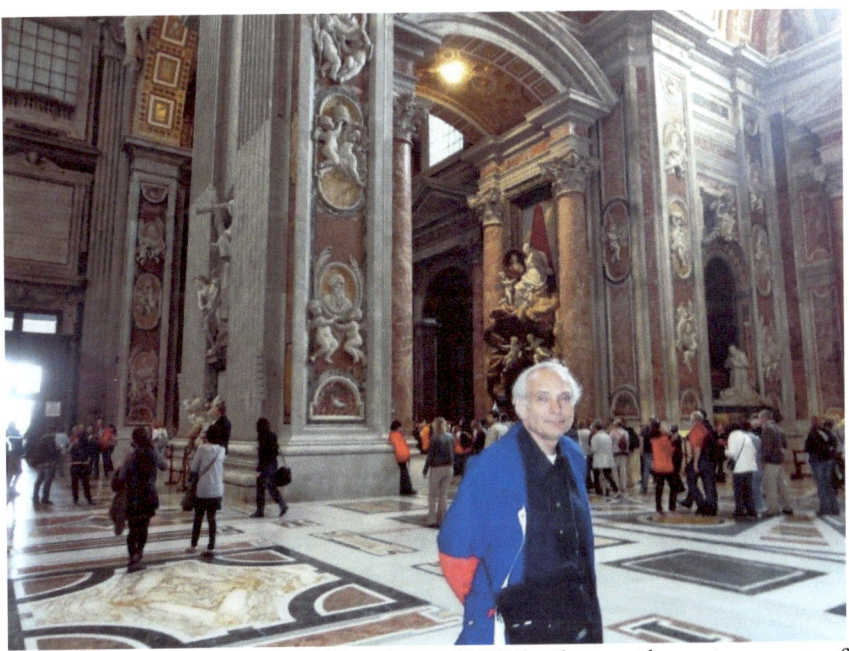

Rome (753 BC), Vatican City State (1929): the south-eastern part of the nave of the Basilica di San Pietro (1506 – 1626,), designed by Michelangelo and finished by Maderno, the entrance is on left.

1627 – Rembrandt, 21, painted The Flight into Egypt, The Rich Man from the Parable, The apostle Paul in Prison.

1628 – Rembrandt, 22, is regularly mentioned as a painter from this year on.

14 February - the 14.8-year-old Gerrit Dou (7 April 1613 – 9 Feb 1675, aged 61.8) becomes Rembrandt's first pupil. Isaac Jouderville also works with Rembrandt.

Rembrandt makes two etchings of an old woman, probably his mother, as well as several undated self-portraits.

He painted Simeon in the Temple, The Foot Operation, Rembrandt Laughing, Self-Portrait Study in the Mirror (the Human Skin), Lighting Study in the Mirror, Bust of a Man Wearing a Turban, Interior with figures, called 'La main chaude', The Painter in his Studio ('Idea'), Two Old Men Disputing (St. Peter and St. Paul).

1629 – Rembrandt was 23 when his older brother Adriaan, 32, and his wife Lijsbeth Simons van Leeuwen had a daughter Cornelia Ariens van Rijn.

Rembrandt completed a painted self-portrait, his earliest dated picture of himself. The same year he signs and dates an etched self-portrait.

Rembrandt never went abroad, but he was considerably influenced by the work of the Italian masters (especially Leonardo da Vinci, Michelangelo and Raphael) and by Netherlandish artists who had studied in Italy, like Flemish Peter Paul Rubens.

After his stay in the northern Netherlands in this year, Ambassador Sir Robert Kerr, 51, (1578 - 1654, aged 76), later the first Earl of Ancrum, gives several paintings to King Charles I, among them 'the picture done by Rembrandt, being his own picture & done by himself'.

The stateman Sir Constantijn Huygens, 34, (4 Sep 1596 – 28 March 1687, aged 90.5, poet and composer, also father of the future mathematician Christaan Huygens, now a few months old, (14 April 1629 – 8 July 1695, aged 66.2, founder of mathematical physics, contributions in optics and mechanics, discovered Saturn's moon Titan, invention of the Huygenian eyepiece for the telescope, and invented the pendulum clock in 1656, which was a breakthrough in timekeeping and became the most accurate timekeeper for almost

300 years), secretary to Stadholder Frederick Henry, 45, (29 Jan 1584 – 14 March 1647, aged 63.1), visits the Leiden studio shared by Rembrandt and Jan Lievens, 22, and compares their work. He finds them both brilliant, but too introverted. Not long afterwards, Huygens procures Rembrandt important commissions from the court of The Hague. Prince Frederik Hendrik continued to purchase paintings from Rembrandt for 17 years, until 1646.

Rembrandt painted Judas Repentant, Returning the Pieces of Silver, The Supper at Emmaus, An Old Man Asleep by the Fire (perhaps typifying 'Sloth'), The apostle Paul at his Writing Desk, Self-portrait with Plumed Beret, Self-portrait with a Gorget, Self-portrait Lit from the Left, Bust of an Old Man Wearing a Fur Cap.

1630 – 27 April - Rembrandt was 23.8 when his father, Harmen Gerritszoon van Rijn passed away at 62 (1568 – 27 April 1630, the river Rijn).

Rembrandt painted Self-portrait with Beret and Gathered Shirt ('stilus mediocris'), Bust of an Old Woman at Prayer ('stilus gravis'), Laughing Soldier ('stilus humilis'), Bust of an Old Man, Samson Betrayed by Delilah, David Playing the Harp for King Saul, Jeremiah Lamenting the Destruction of Jerusalem, Andromeda, The Good Samaritan, Oil Study of an Old Man, Oil Study of an Old Man (2), Bust of an Old Man.

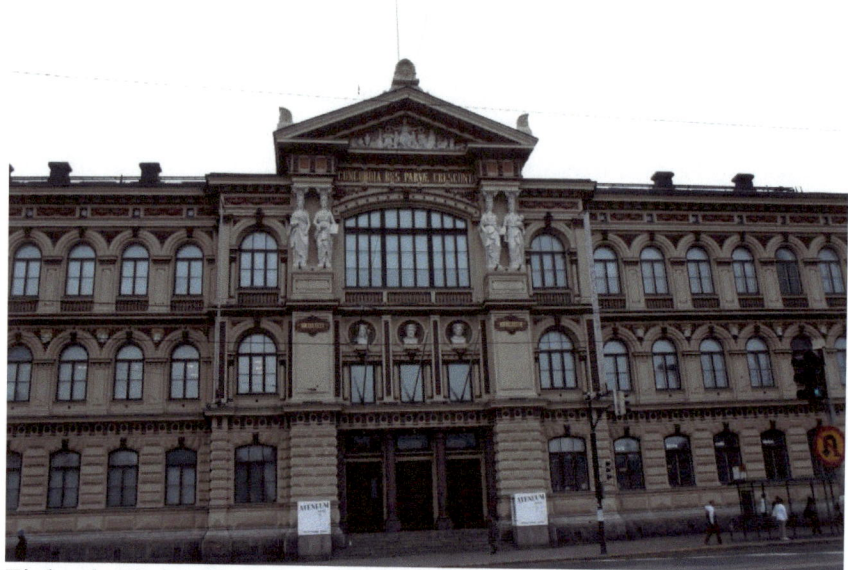

Finland, Helsinki: The Ateneum (1887). Center busts: Rafael, Phidias, and Bramante. Right: Benvenutto Cellini, Tessin. Left: Michelangelo, Rubens, Thorwaldsen, Rembrandt, Toesergel.

1631 – 8 March - Rembrandt was 24.6 when his oldest brother Gerrit Harmenszoon van Rijn, 40.5, had a son Ruggertson Garretson born in Baltimore, Maryland, English American colonies.

20 September – Rembrandt was 25.1 when his oldest brother Gerrit Harmenszoon van Rijn passed away at 41 (1590 – 20 Sep 1631, had a son Ruggertson Garretson born on 8 March 1631 in Baltimore, Maryland, English American colonies, just 6.5 months old).

Rembrandt, 25, commutes to Amsterdam (which was expanding as the new business capital of the Netherlands), stays at the house of the influential art dealer Hendrick Uylenburgh (c. 1587 – 1661, aged c. 74), and used studio space there to practice as a professional portraitist for the first time, with great success (also for the painting The Anatomy Lesson of Dr. Tulp). (Rembrandt lends him 1000 guilders (circa $30,000)). At the end of the year he moved to Amsterdam.

He painted St. Peter in Prison, Simeon in the Temple, The Abduction of Proserpina, An Old Woman Reading, probably the Prophetess Anna, Christ on the Cross, The Artist in an Oriental

Costume, with a Poodle at his Feet, Minerva in her Study, Bust of an Old Man with a Cap and Gold Chain, A Man Wearing a Gorget and Plumed Cap, Half-figure of a Man Wearing a Gorget and Plumed Hat, Portrait of Nicolaes Ruts, Portrait of a Man at a Writing Desk, possibly Jacob Bruyningh, A Scholar Near a Window (a study in 'kamerlicht').

<u>1632</u> – Rembrandt was 26 when "Treatise on Painting by Leonardo da Vinci" was published in France – contained Leonardo's work on the studies of anatomy, light and the landscape, which were assembled for publication by his pupil Francesco Melzi. In France went into 62 editions in fifty years.

Rembrandt painted The Raising of Lazarus, The Rape of Europa (inspired from Ovidius' Metamorphoses), A Lady and Gentleman in Black, Portrait of a Man, Portrait of a Woman, Portrait of a Man, probably a Member of the Van Beresteyn Family, Portrait of a Woman, probably a Member of the Van Beresteyn Family, Portrait of a Man Trimming his Quill, Portrait of a Woman Seated, Portrait of Princess Amalia van Solms, Self-portrait as a Burger, Portrait of Maurits Huygens, Portrait of Jacques de Gheyn III, Self-portrait, Portrait of Joris de Caullery, Portrait of a Young Man, Portrait of Marten Looten, Portrait of a 40-year-old Man, Portrait of a 39-year-old Woman, Portrait of a 62-year-old Woman, possibly Aeltje Pietersdr Uylenburgh, The Anatomy Lesson of Dr. Tulp, Portraits of Jean Pellicorne and his Son Casper, Portraits of Susanna van Collen and her Daughter Anna, Bust of a Young Woman, Bust of a Young Woman in a Cap, Half-figure of a Young Woman in Profile with a Fan, Bearded Old Man, Study of an Old Man with a Gold Chain, The Apostle Peter, Knee-length Figure of a Man in an Oriental Dress ('The Noble Slav'), Interior with a Window and a Winding Staircase (a study in 'kamerlicht').

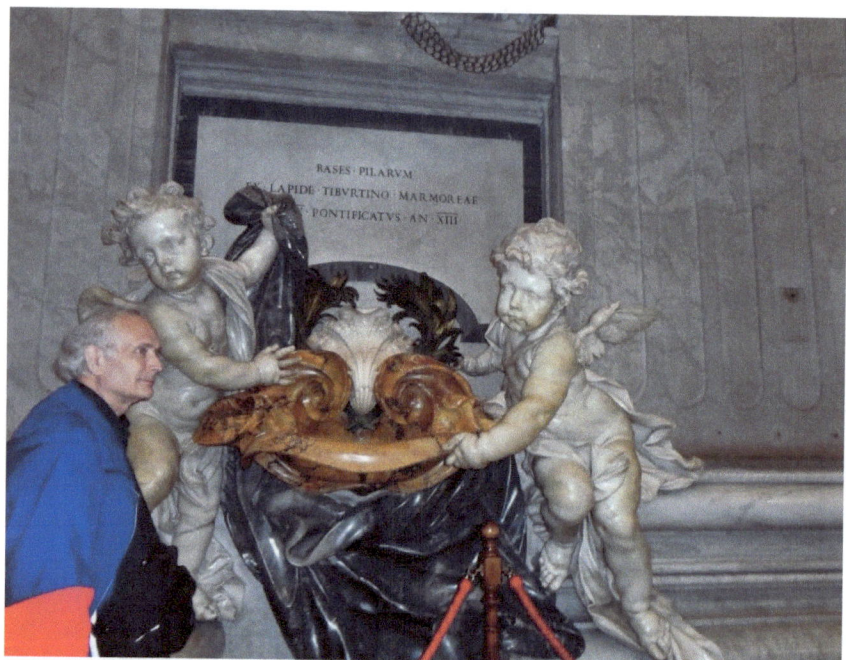

Rome (753 BC), Vatican City State (1929): the south-eastern part of the nave of the Basilica di San Pietro (1506 – 1626,), designed by Michelangelo and finished by Maderno, with a Holy Water basin having two cherubs (2 m) who flutter against the first pier.

1633 – Rembrandt, 27, painted Portrait of a Man Rising from his Chair, Portrait of a Young Woman with a Fan, Portrait of Jan Rijcksen and his Wife Griet Jans, Portrait of Johannes Wtenbogaert, Portrait of Man, Portrait of a Man Wearing a Red Doublet, Portrait of a Young Woman, Bust of Saskia Smiling, Half-length Portrait of Saskia van Uylenburgh, Self-portrait with Gold Chain, Self-portrait with Beret and Gold Chain, Bust of Young Woman, Man in Oriental Costume, A Young Woman (Esther? Judith?) at her Toilet, Bellona, Daniel Refuses to Worship the Idol Baal, A Bust of an Old Man, Bust of a Man in Oriental Dress, Christ in the Storm on the Sea of Galilee, The Raising of the Cross, The Descent from the Cross, The Adoration of the Magi, Portrait of a 41-year-old Man, possibly Pieter Sijen.

5 June - Rembrandt, 26.8, marries Saskia van Uylenburgh, 20.9, (2 August 1612 – 14 June 1642, aged 29.9) at Sint Annaparochie in Friesland. She was the cousin of Rembrandt's

landlord, and the daughter of the late burgomaster (mayer) of Leeuwarden. They lived in the house of H. Uylenburgh

8 June – Rembrandt finished his drawing "Portrait of Saskia as a Bride", silver pen on white-grounded parchment, 18.5 cm x 10.6 cm, on which he wrote (translated): "This was portrayed after my wife when she was 21 years old, the third day after we were married. June 8, 1633".

1634 – Rembrandt, 28, becomes an Amsterdam citizen, and joins the local St Luke's guild of painters. He also had several students, including Ferdinand Bol, 18, (24 June 1616 – 24 August 1680, aged 64 years and 2 months, Dutch painter, etcher and draftsman), and Govert Flinck, 19, (25 Jan 1615 – 2 Feb 1660, aged 45 years and 8 days, Duth painter).

He painted Joseph Telling his Dreams, John the Baptist Preaching, Christ and his Disciples in Gethsemane, Ecce Homo, The Lamentation, Portrait of a Young Bachelor, Portrait of an 83-year Old Woman (possibly Aechje Claesdr, mother of Dirck Jansz Pesser), Portrait of Dirck Jansz Pesser, Portret of van Haesje Jacobsdr van Cleyburgh, Portrait of a Man in a Broad-brimmed Hat, Portrait of a Woman, Portrait of a 40-year-old Woman, possibly Marretje Cornelisdr van Grotewal, Portrait of Maerten Soolmans, Portrait of Oopjen Coppit, Portrait of Reverend Johannes Elison, Portrait of Maria Bockenolle, Oval Self-portrait with Shaded Eyes, Self-portrait in a Cap and Fur-trimmed Cloak, Flora, The Descent from the Cross, The Incredulity of Thomas, Sophonisba Receiving the Poisoned Cup, A Scholar, Seated at a Table with Books, Diana Bathing with her Nymphs, with the Stories of Actaeon and Callisto, The Flight into Egypt, The Holy Family.

He finished the drawing "The Last Supper, after Leonardo da Vinci", red chalk, 36.2 cm x 47.5 cm.

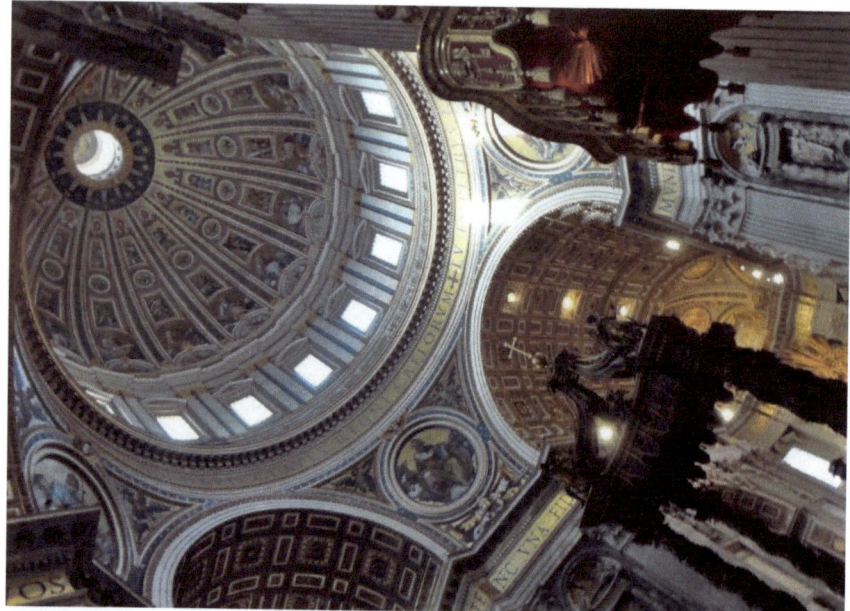

Rome (753 BC), Vatican City State (1929): interior of the Basilica Papale di San Pietro (1506 – 1626,), the dome (left, 137 m height (the tallest dome in the world), 42 m diameter, with Michelangelo's ideas), baldacchino (right down, 30 m, Bernini).

1635 – Rembrandt, 29, and his wife Saskia moved into his own rented house, in stylish Nieuwe Doelenstraat.

He painted Bust of a Young Man Wearing a Plumed Cap, Portrait of Philips Lucasz, Portrait of Petronella Buys, Portrait of a Man in a Slouched Hat and Bandoleer, Portrait of a Young Woman, Self-portrait wearing a white feathered bonnet, Self-portrait as the Prodigal Son in the Tavern (with his wife Saskia, 23), Abraham's Sacrifice, The Rape of Ganymede, Flora, Minerva, Samson Threatening his Father-in-law, Bust of a Man in Oriental Dress, Bust of a Bearded Old man in Fanciful Costume, Belshazzar's Feast.

He finished two drawings "The Last Supper, after Leonardo da Vinci", first red chalk, heightened with white, on paper, 12.5 cm x 21 cm, and second pen and brown ink, wash, traces of white, 12.8 cm x 38.5 cm.

15 December – Rembrandt (29 years and 5 months) and his wife Saskia (23.3) had their first child Rombertus baptized in Amsterdam.

1636 – 15 February – Rembrandt's (29 years and 7 months) and his wife Saskia's (23.4) first child Rombertus passed away at the age of 2 months, and was buried in Amsterdam.

Rembrandt, 30, painted Susanna Bathing, The Ascension, Self-portrait Transformed into a 'tronie', The Standard-Bearer, The Blinding of Samson, Danaë (from Greek mythology – the mother of Perseus).

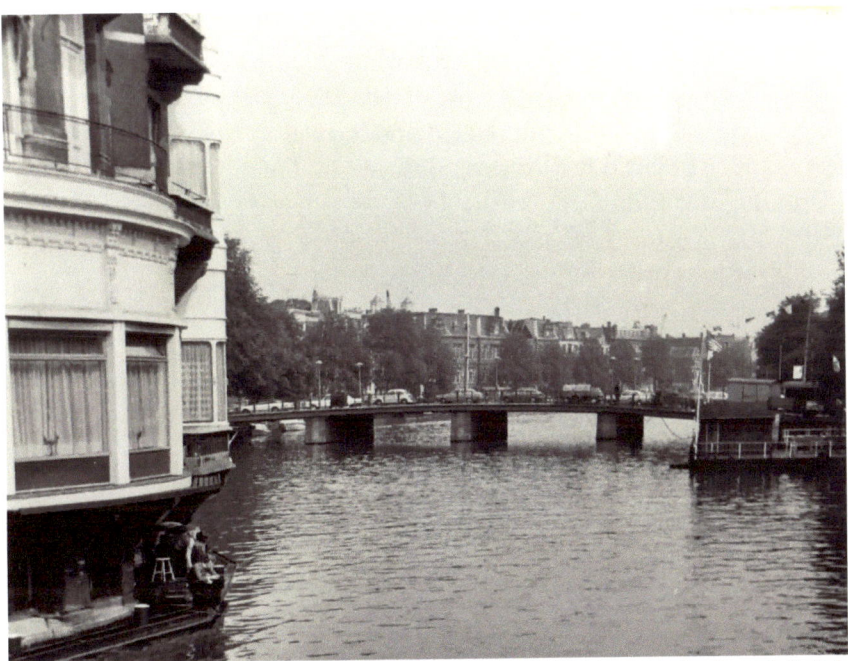

Netherlands, 14 Aug 1977, Amsterdam (1275, population 1.3 M, elevation minus 2 m (2 m under the Atlantic Ocean level)): Zijkanaal G, with a bridge for the street s150, and Havenstraat on the left.

1637 – Rembrandt, 31, moves again into the "Rembrandt house" in the Anthonisbreestraat.

He painted The Angel Raphael Leaving Tobit and his Family, The Parable of the Labourers in the Vineyard, River Landscape with Ruins, The Concord of the State, Self-portrait, A Polish Nobleman, Portrait of the Preacher Eleazar Swalmius, Bust of a Man with Plumed Cap.

1638 – 22 July - Rembrandt (32 years and 7 days) and his wife Saskia (25.9) had their second child Cornelija baptized in Amsterdam.

13 August - Rembrandt's (32 years and 29 days) and his wife Saskia's (26 years and 11 days) second child Cornelija passed away at the age of 22 days, and was buried in Amsterdam

Rembrandt painted The Risen Christ Appearing to Mary Magdalene, Landscape with the Good Samaritan, The Wedding of Samson, Woman with a Mirror.

1639 – Rembrandt was 33 when his older brother Cornelis passed away at circa 43 (c 1594 – c 1639).

He and his wife purchased and moved to a newly built house (now the Rembrandt House Museum) in the upscale 'Breestraat' ('Broadway'), today known as Jodenbreestraat (Jodenbreestraat 4, 1011 NK Amsterdam-now). The mortgage to finance the 13,000 guilder (circa $400,000) purchase would be a primary cause for later financial difficulties. Rembrandt should easily have been able to pay the house off with his large income, but his spending was too much, and he also made some unsuccessful investments.

Rembrandt painted The Entombment, The Resurrection, King Uzziah Stricken with Leprosy, Two Dead Peacocks and a Girl, A Dead Bittern, Portrait of a Man Standing, possibly Andries de Graeff, Portrait of Aletta Adriaensdr, Self-portrait.

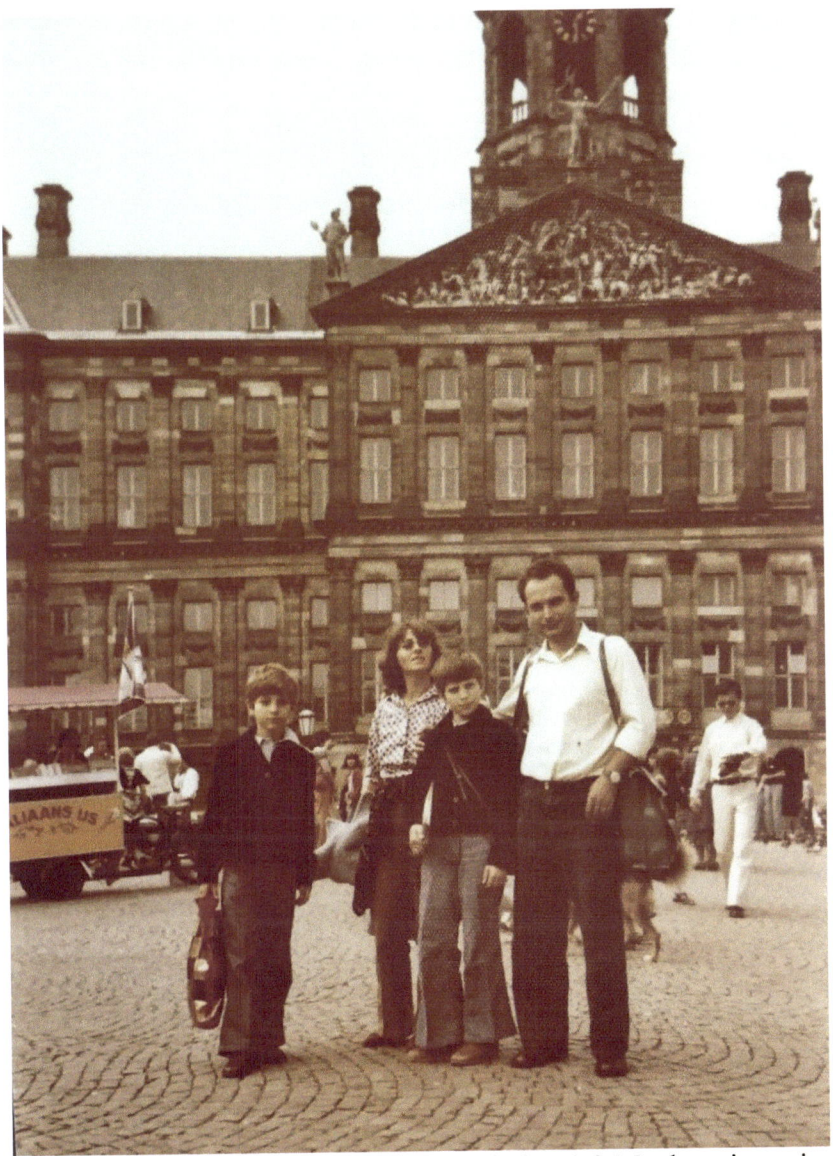

14 Aug 1977, Amsterdam (1275, population 1.3 M, elevation minus 2 m (2 m under the Atlantic Ocean), 360 km west of Göttingen): the east façade of the Royal Palace (1655 (initially Town Hall, inspired by Roman palaces, first king Louis Napoleon (1778-1846, King of Holland 1806-1810, a younger brother of Napoleon)) built on 13,659 wooden piles (like in Venezia), floor area 22,031 m^2, with yellowish sandstone from Bentheim in Germany), on the west side of Dam Square.

1640 – Rembrandt was 34 when his mother, Neeltgen Willemsdochter van Zuijtbrouck, passed away at 72 (1568 – 1640); she was the daughter of a baker, and a Roman Catholic. With her husband, she had 10 children, two died in infancy. Rembrandt, 34, was the 9th child. Now 4 children were still living: Adriaan (shoemaker), Willem (baker), Rembrandt, and the youngest child - daughter Lijsbeth.

30 May – Rembrandt was 33.8 when Sir Peter Paul Rubens died (28 June 1577 – 30 May 1640, aged 62.9, great Flemish painter, 387 paintings and drawings, father of eight children (3 with his first wife Isabella, and 5 with his second wife Helena)).

29 July - Rembrandt (34 years and 14 days) and his wife Saskia (4 days before 28) had their third child Cornelija baptized in Amsterdam.

12 August - Rembrandt's (34 years and 28 days) and his wife Saskia's (28 and 10 days) second child Cornelija passed away at the age of 14 days, and was buried in Amsterdam.

Rembrandt painted Portrait of a Man Holding a Hat, Self-portrait, Bust of Young Woman, The Holy Family with St Anne, The Visitation, Landscape with a Stone Bridge, Mountain Landscape with Approaching Storm, Portrait of Herman Doomer, Portrait of Baertje Martens, Self-portrait, Self-Portrait at the Age of 34, Oil Study of a Woman Lit Obliquely from Behind.

1641 – 4 September - Rembrandt (35.1) and his wife Saskia (29.08) had their fourth child Titus born, and on 22 Sep baptized in Amsterdam. They had 4 children, but 3 died shortly after birth.

Rembrandt painted Portrait of a Woman, possibly Anna Wijmer, Saskia as a Flora, Portrait of the Mennonite Preacher Cornelius Claesz Anslo and his Wife Aaltje Gerritsdr Shouten, Portrait of Maria Trip, A Scholar at a Writing Desk, Girl in Fanciful Costume in a Picture Frame, Portrait of Nicolas van Bambeeck in a Picture Frame, Portrait of Agatha Bas in a Picture Frame.

1642 – 14 June - Rembrandt was 35.9 when his wife Saskia passed away at 29 years, 10 months, and 12 days, (9 years and 9 days after marriage), probably from tuberculosis. Rembrandt's drawings of his wife on her sick and death bed are among his most touching works.

Rembrandt employs Geertje Dircks, c. 30, (c. 1612 – c. 1656, aged c. 44), a trumpeter's widow, as nanny for the 9 months and 10 days old son Titus. Rembrandt begins a relationship with her.

Rembrandt painted David's Parting from Jonathan, Self-Portrait, The Company of Captain Frans Banning Cocq and Lieutenant Willem van Ruytenburch (Night Watch).

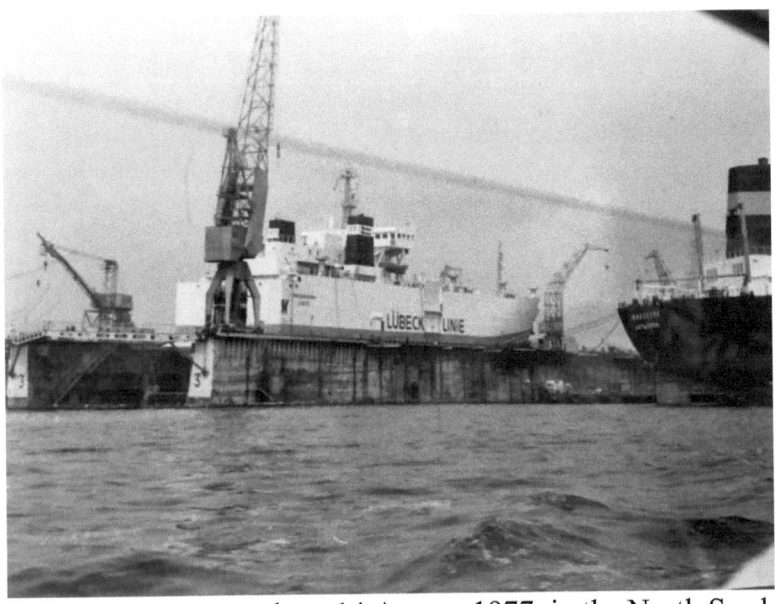

Netherlands, Amsterdam, 14 August 1977, in the North See harbor two big ships: Lübeck Linie (center), Naaskerk Antwerpen (right).

1643 – Rembrandt, 37, painted Portrait of a Man with a Hawk, Portrait of a Woman with a Fan, An Old Man in Rich Costume (Boaz?), Bust of a Woman (Ruth?), Sarah Waiting for Tobias.

1644 – Rembrandt, 38, painted Portrait of a Man with a Steel Gorget, Christ and the Woman Taken in Adultery, A Weeping Woman.

1645 – Rembrandt, 39, painted The Holy Family with Angels, Self-portrait with Beret and Red Cloak, Girl Leaning on a Stone Window Sill, Tobit and Anna, Joseph's Dream in the Stable at Bethlehem, Old Man with Fur Coat, Old Man with a Stick, The Mill.

1646 – Rembrandt, 40, painted Winter Landscape, Abraham Serving the Three Angels, The Holy Family with Painted Frame and Curtain, The Prophetess Anna in the Temple, The Nativity, Saul and David.

1647 – Rembrandt was 41 when Hendrickje Stoffels, 21, (1926 – 21 July 1663, aged 37) joins household as maidservant.
Rembrandt painted Susanna and the Elders (from the Bible), Nocturnal Landscape with the Holy Family, Preparatory Oil Sketch for the Etched Portrait of Dr. Ephraim Bueno.

1648 – Rembrandt, 42, painted Portrait of a Man Reading by Candlelight, Oil Study of Christ, Oil Study of Christ, The Supper at Emmaus.

1649 – Rembrandt, 43, and Dircks, 37. had problems, because she expected him to marry her, and Rembrandt was ordered to pay maintenance allowance of 200 guilders (circa $6,000)/year.

1650 – Rembrandt, 44, painted Christ Appearing to Mary Magdalene, 'Noli me tangere', and a Self-Portrait.

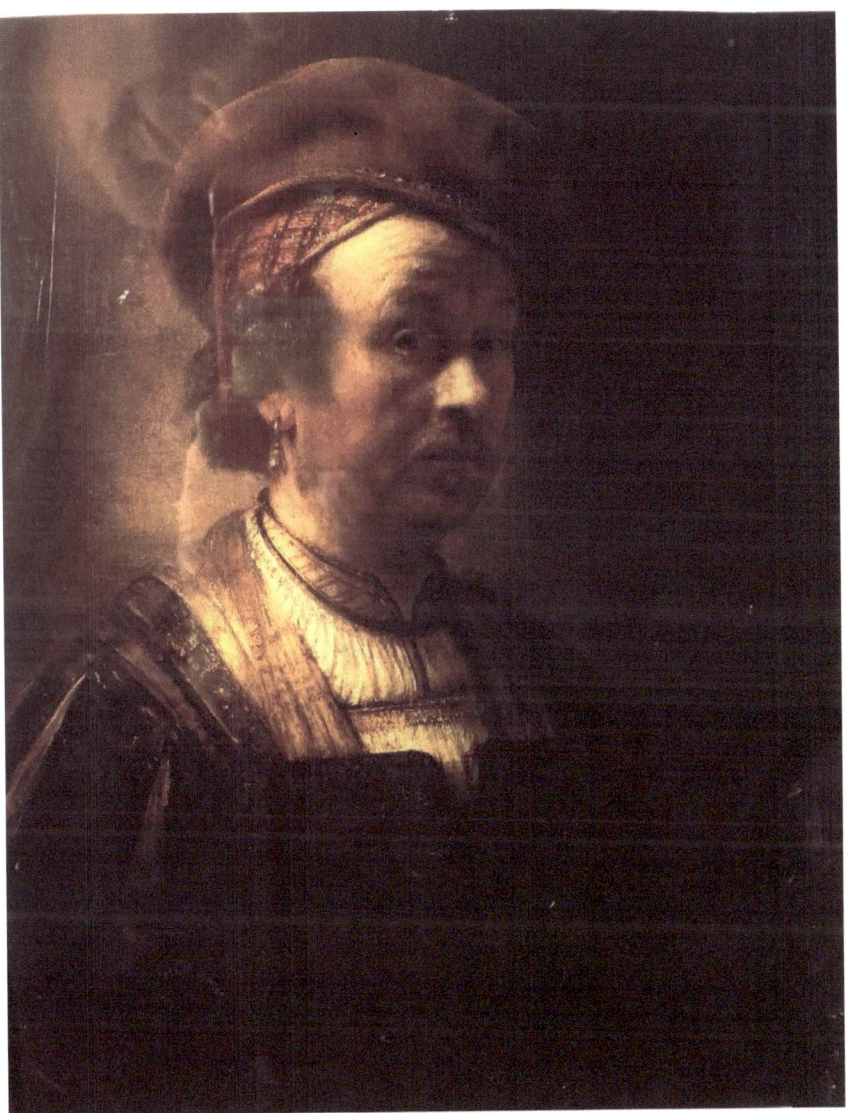
Rembrandt, 44, 1650, Self-Portrait.

1651 – Rembrandt was 45 when "Treatise on Painting by Leonardo da Vinci" was published in Italy – contained Leonardo's work on the studies of anatomy, light and the landscape, which were assembled for publication by his pupil Francesco Melzi.
Rembrandt painted Girl at a Window, An Old Man in Fanciful Costume, Portrait of a Man.

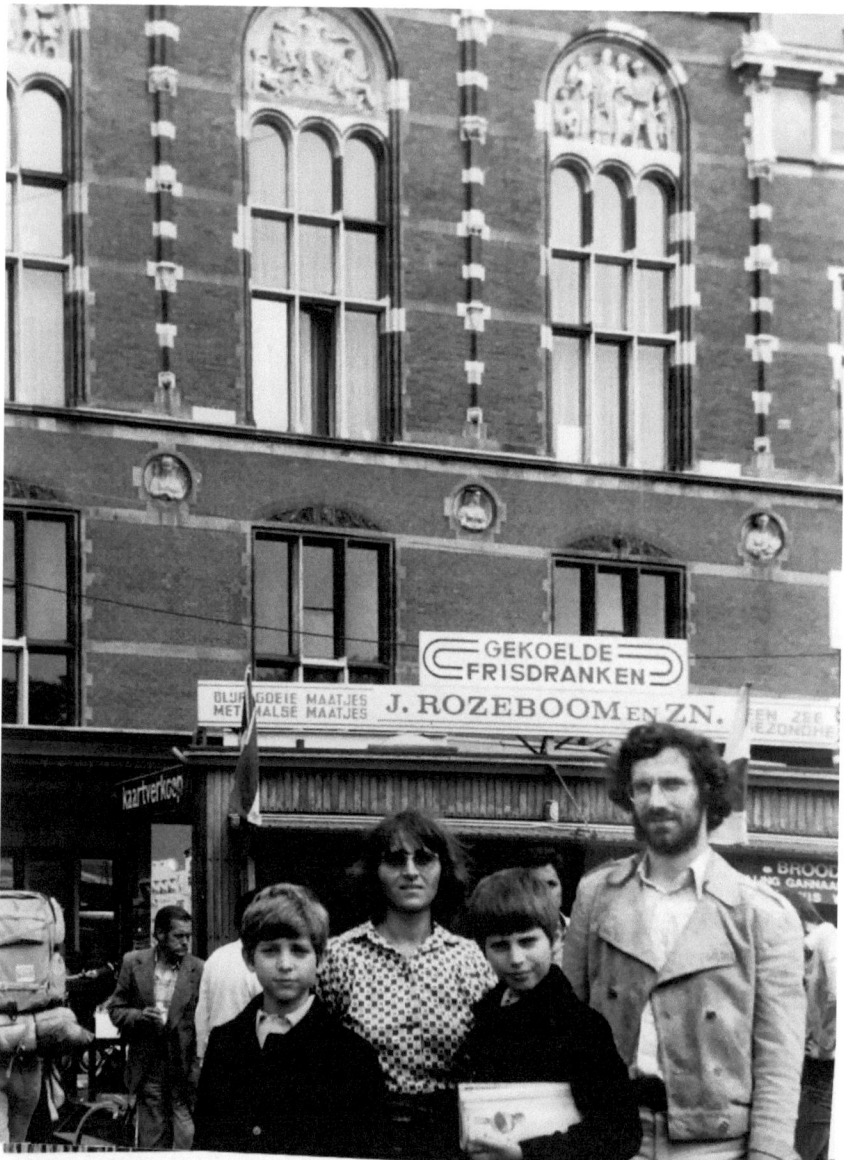

Netherlands, 14 Aug 1977, Amsterdam (1275, population 1.3 M, elevation minus 2 m (2 m under the Atlantic Ocean level)), near a petit restaurant on Rozenboomsteeg, near the Amsterdam Museum (1926, a museum about the history of Amsterdam) and Universiteitsbibliotheek Singel (the library of the University of Amsterdam and the Academic Medical Center, is in the town center at Singel, close to Heiligeweg and Koningsplein).

1652 – 19 December - Rembrandt's (46) older brother Adriaan Harmenszoon van Rijn passed away at 55 (1597 – 1652). Adriaan, 20, married Lijsbeth Simons van Leeuwen on 2 February 1617, and had a daughter Cornelia Ariens van Rijn born in 1629, when Adriaan was 32.

Rembrandt painted Hendrickje with Fur Wrap, The So-called Large Vienna Self-portrait with Beret, Portrait of Nicolaes Bruyningh.

1653 – Rembrandt, 47, painted Half-figure of a Bearded Man with Beret, Aristotle with a Bust of Homer.

1654 – 30 October - Rembrandt, 48, had his fifth child, an illegitimate daughter, Cornelia (30 Oct 1654 – 1684, aged 30), with Hendrickje Stoffels, 28, (1626 – 1663, aged 37).

Rembrandt had all his five children christened in Dutch Reformed churches in Amsterdam: four in the Oude Kerk (Old Church) and one, Titus, in the Zuiderkerk (Southern Church).

He painted A Woman Wading in a Pool (Callisto in the Wilderness), Oil Study of an Old Man with a Red Hat, Bathsheba at her Toilet (from the Bible), Woman at an Open Half-door, Portrait of Jan Six, The Standard-Bearer (Floris Soop), Self-portrait, Portrait of Hendrickje Stoffels.

1655 – 26 August - Rembrandt was 49.1 when his older brother Willem passed away at circa 56 (c 1599 – 26 August 1655).

28 October – Rembrandt was 49.2 when his younger sister Lysbeth van Rijn passed away at circa 47 (circa 1608 – 28 Oct 1655).

Rembrandt painted The Polish Rider, Joseph Accused by Potiphar's Wife, Oil Sketch of an Old Man, Man in Armour, Slaughtered Ox, Old Woman Reading (Study in Lighting Effects), Titus at a Desk (Portrait of Titus van Rijn, 14, (1641-1668, aged 27), Rembrandt's son with Saskia van Uylenburgh.).

1656 – Rembrandt, 50, lived beyond his means, buying art (Old Master paintings and drawings, included busts of the Roman Emperors, and including bidding up his own work), prints (often used in his paintings) and rarities (suits of Japanese armor among many objects from Asia, and collections of natural history and minerals), which probably caused a court arrangement to avoid his bankruptcy this year, by selling most of his paintings and large collection of antiquities.

He transferred his house to his son Titus, 15, in order to save his inheritance. The liquidation of Rembrandt's property begins. Inventory of goods was taken. Rembrandt couldn't remarry because he would risk losing income from Saskia's estate. The reason given for liquidation was "losses in business as well as damage and losses at sea." It was explained by some - maybe he invested in cargo that was lost at sea, or his pictures were lost at sea.

Rembrandt painted Unfinished Portrait of a Boy, Man with Beret and Tabard (a Falconer?), Jacob Blessing the Sons of Joseph, The Anatomy Lesson of Dr. Jan Deyman, Young Man Seated at a Table, Portrait of a Gentleman with a Pair of Gloves, Portrait of a Lady with an Ostrich Feather Fan, Portrait of a Man, possibly Arnout Tholincx, Portrait of poet Jeremias de Decker.

The Dutch mathematician Christaan Huygens, 27, invented the pendulum clock, which was a breakthrough in timekeeping, and became the most accurate timekeeper for almost 300 years).

1657 – Rembrandt, 51, noticed that the prices realized in the sales this year were disappointing.

He painted Venus and Cupid, Juno, Pallas Athena, The Apostle Paul at his Writing Desk, The Apostle Bartholomew, The So-called Small Vienna Self-portrait, Portrait of Titus van Rijn, Portrait of Catharina Hooghsaet.

1658 – May - Rembrandt, 51.9, noticed that the prices realized in the sales this year were disappointing. He was forced to sell his house at St. Anthonisbreestraat and his printing-press.

He moved with Hendrickje, 32, Titus, 16.6, and Cornelia, 3.6, moved to a more modest rented house in Rozengracht (now no. 184) in the Jordaan district of Amsterdam, opposite the Nieuwe Doolhof (the maze).

Rembrandt paints himself seated in state like a monarch.

In an etched self portrait of the artist at work as an etcher. It is his last self-portrait in this medium.

Rembrandt, painted Portrait of an Unknown Scholar (also known as 'The Auctioneer'), Preparatory Oil Sketch for the Etched Portrait of Lieven Willemsz van Coppenol, Portrait of a Man with Arms Akimbo, The Risen Christ, Portrait of Dirck van Os, Self-portrait, Philemon and Baucis.

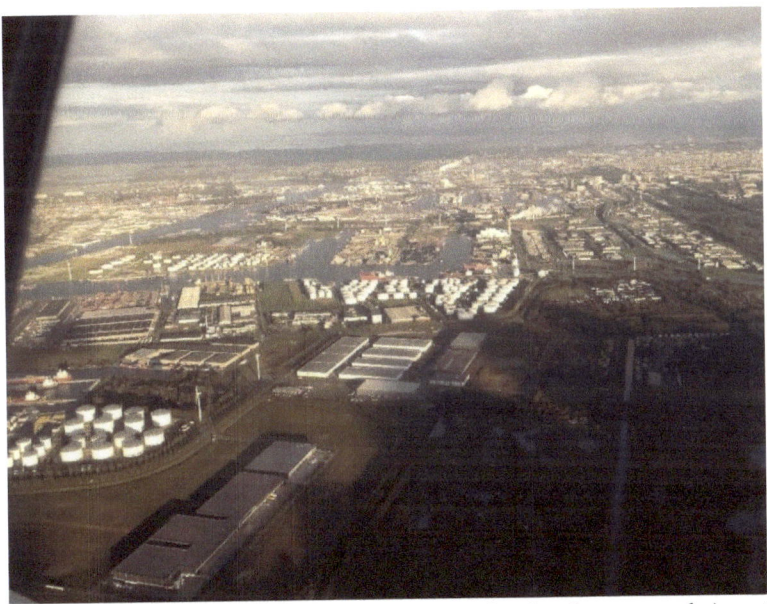

View from airplane of part of The Netherlands, around Amsterdam (1306) Airport Schiphol (1916, 3 m under the Atlantic Ocean level).

1659 – Rembrandt, 53, painted Tobit and Anna, Moses Smashes the Stone Tablets with the Covenant (unfinished), Jacob Wrestling with the Angel, Portrait of a Man as the Apostle Paul, Oil Sketch for 'Portrait Historié' of an Unknown Gentleman as St Bavo, 'Portrait Historié' of an Unknown Gentleman as St Bavo, Self-portrait, Self Portrait with Beret and Turned-Up Collar, Self-portrait (unfinished), Lighting Study with an Old Man as a Model, Lighting Study with Hendrickje Stoffels in a Silk Gown as a Model.

1660 – The Amsterdam painters' guild introduced a new rule that no one in Rembrandt's circumstances could trade as a painter.
15 December – To get around this, Hendrickje, 34, and Titus, 19.2, set up a business as art dealers (trade in paintings, graphic art, engravings and woodcuts), with Rembrandt, 54.4 as an employee,

thus relieving him of all financial control. He can continue to paint, but must leave business matters to them. Titus becomes universal heir.

Rembrandt painted Posthumous Portrait of Saskia van Uylenburgh as Flora, Hendrickje Stoffels, Titus van Rijn as St Francis, A Smiling Young Man (Titus), Self-portrait at an Easel, Rembrandt: Self Portrait, Assuerus, Haman, and Esther, The Denial of Peter.

1661 – Rembrandt was 55 when the new business (where his former maid Hendrickje, 35, and his son Titus, 20, were now his bosses) was contracted to complete work for the newly built city hall, but only after Rembrandt's apprentice (26 years ago) Govert Flinck, the artist previously commissioned, died on 2 Feb 1660, aged 45 years and 8 days, without beginning to paint. The resulting work, The Conspiracy of Claudius Civilis (1662), was rejected and returned to the painter; the surviving fragment is only a fraction of the whole work. It was around this time that Rembrandt took on his last apprentice, Aert de Gelder, 16, (26 Oct 1645 – 27 August 1727, aged 81.8, Dutch painter), for two years, until 1663.

Rembrandt, 55, painted Lighting Study of an Old Man in Profile, The Circumcision in the Stable, The Virgin of Sorrow, Titus Posing for a Study of an Angel, St. Matthew and the Angel, The Apostle Bartholomew, The Apostle Simon, The Apostle James the Greater, The Apostle James the Less, or Christ with a Staff, Self-portrait as the Apostle Paul, Two Moors, The Small Margaretha de Geer, Portrait of Jacob Trip, Portrait of Margaretha de Geer.

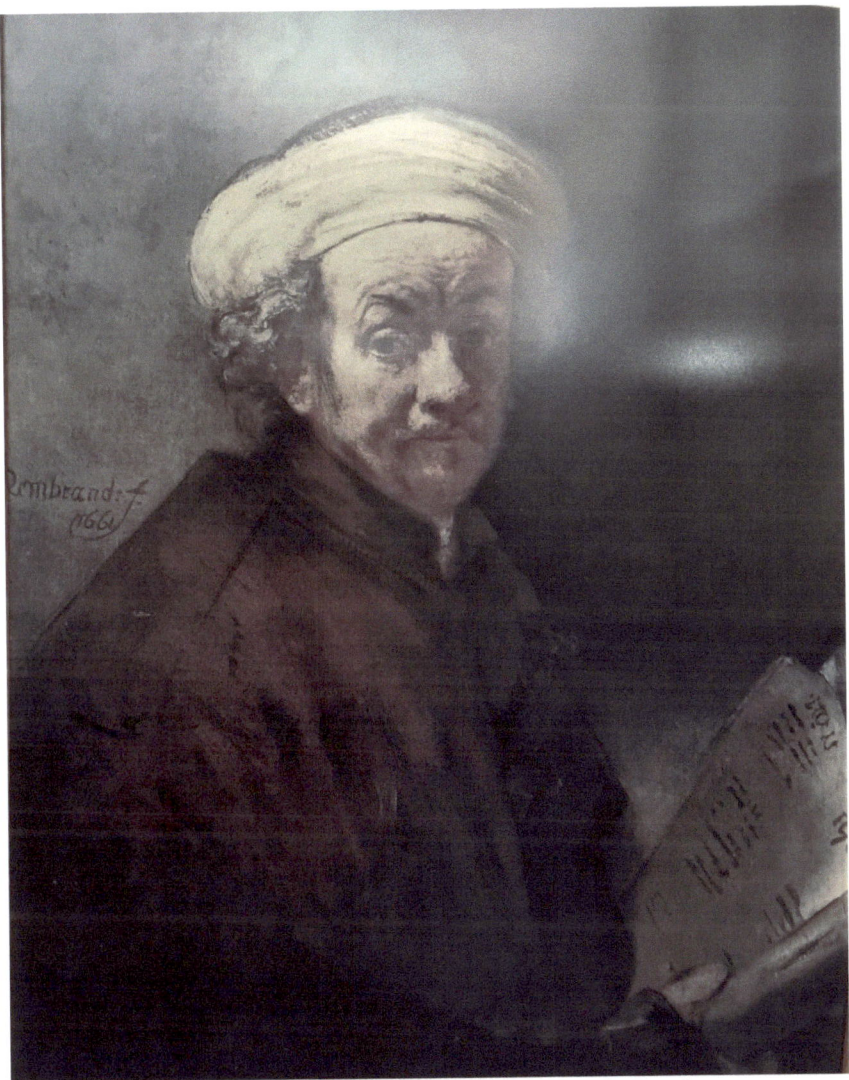

Rembrandt, 55, 1661, Self-portrait as the Apostle Paul

1662 – Rembrandt, 56, painted The Conspiracy of the Batavians under Claudius Civilis, Portrait of the Syndics of the Amsterdam Clothmakers' Guild, known as the 'Staalmeesters', Portrait of a Young Man.

He received major commissions for portraits and other works, some from the wealthy Trip family.

1663 – Rembrandt was 57 when Hendrickje Stoffels died at 37, probably a victim of the plague which hit Amsterdam.

24 July -She was buried in a rented grave in Amsterdam's Westerkerkon.

Rembrandt painted Homer Dictating his Verses, Self-portrait as the Laughing Zeuxis while Painting an Old Woman, Equestrian Portrait of Frederick Rihe, Bust of a Bearded Young Man with a Skullcap.

1664 – 21 July – Rembrandt was 58 when the painter Christiaen Dusart, 46, (1618 – 1682, aged 64) is appointed guardian of Cornelia van Rijn, 9.7. Her father, Rembrandt, is described as 'hale and hearty', in full use of his mind, memory and speech'.

The learned Swiss monk Gabriel Bucelimis, 65, (1599 – 1681, aged 82), notes in his diary that Rembrandt is 'the miracle of our age (Rimprant, nostrae aetatis miraculum)'.

Rembrandt painted Titus Reading (study in direct and reflected light), The Return of the Prodigal Son.

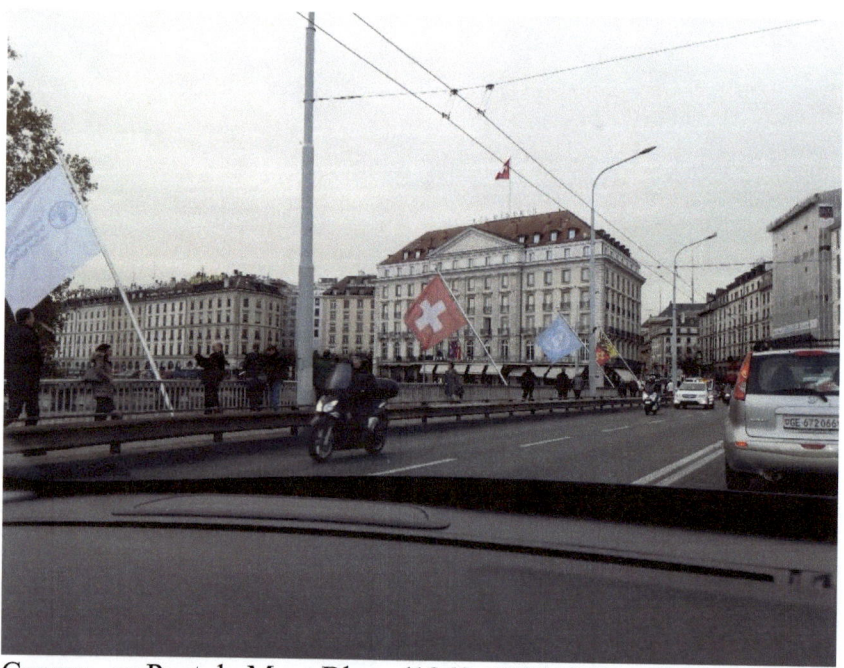

Geneva, on Pont du Mont Blanc (1862, 1965, 252 m X 26.8 m, over Rhône river), going northwest, Les Bergues Hotel (1834) (center).

1665 – 21 March - Rembrandt was 58.6 when his son Titus comes of age. Titus van Rijn proudly declares to a Leiden notary: 'Yes, my father cuts (etches) very skillfully.'

19 June - Titus van Rijn applies for and is awarded veniam aetatis (legal maturity).

Rembrandt painted Portrait of a Woman with a Lapdog, Old Man in an Armchair, possibly a portrait of Jan Amos Comenius, Portrait of Gerard de Lairesse, A Presumed Sketch for the Male Sitter in the 'Jewish Bride', Portrait of a Man with a Magnifying Glass, possibly Pieter Haaringh, Portrait of a Woman with a Carnation, possibly Lysbet Jansdr Delft, 'Portrait Historié' of a Couple as Isaac and Rebecca (known as 'The Jewish Bride'), Family Portrait.

1666 – Rembrandt, 60, painted Portrait of Jan Boursse, Sitting by a Stove, Lucretia.

1667 – 29 December – Rembrandt was 61.5 when Cosimo (Cosmvs in Latin) III de' Medici, 25.3, (14 August 1642 – 31 October 1723, aged 81.2, Grand Duke of Tuscany) visited Rembrandt at his house, and then described him as 'pittore Famoso' (famous painter) in his travel journal. It later become known that the Italian Grand Duke of Tuscany owns one of the painter's self-portraits.

Rembrandt painted Portrait of a White-haired Man, Portrait of an Elderly Man Seated, possibly Pieter de la Tombe,

1668 – Rembrandt was 62 when his son Titus, 26.5, marries Magdalena van Loo, 27, (1641 – 1669, aged 28), daughter of a silversmith. The couple lived at Magdalena's mother's house on the Singel.

22 September - Titus died at 27 years and 18 days, and was buried in the Westerkerk in Amsterdam.

Rembrandt was assisted by Cornelia, 13.9, his and Hendrickje's daughter.

Rembrandt painted Portrait of Titus van Rijn, Portrait of a Young Woman, possibly Magdalena van Loo, Self Portrait with Two Circles (unfinished).

1669 – 22 March – Rembrandt was 62.6 when Titia van Rijn (1669 – 1715, aged 46, married François van Bijler in 1686, when she was 17), born a few days before, his granddaughter and goddaughter, was baptized in the Nieuwezijds Chapel, six months after the death of her father Titus.

Rembrandt painted Self-Portrait at the Age of 63, Self-portrait with Beret, Self-portrait, Simeon's Song of Praise (unfinished). Rembrandt created about 86 self-portraits, including over forty paintings, thirty-one etchings, and about seven drawings.

Magdalena van Loo died at 28, and her mother also died, circa 50.

2 October – Rembrandt, 63.2, is visited by the amateur genealogist Pieter van Brederode, 38, (1631 – 1697, aged 66), who makes a record of antiquities and curios in his collection.

4 October - Rembrandt died at 63 years 2 months and 20 days, in Amsterdam.

He was buried in the Westerkerk, in an unknown rented grave. He was survived by his illegitimate daughter Cornelia, 14.9, and his granddaughter Titia van Rijn, 6.5 months.

Rembrandt left 772 paintings (324), drawings and prints.

The French sculptor Auguste Rodin said, "Compare me with Rembrandt! What sacrilege! With Rembrandt, the colossus of Art! We should prostrate ourselves before Rembrandt and never compare anyone with him!"

Many painters said that whenever they see an usual painter, they feel like painting, but whenever they see a Rembrandt, they feel like giving up.

1670 – Bartolomé Esteban Murillo, 53, (31 Dec 1617 – 3 April 1682, aged 64.2, Spanish painter), A Girl and Her Duenna, at the National Gallery of Art in Washington, D.C.

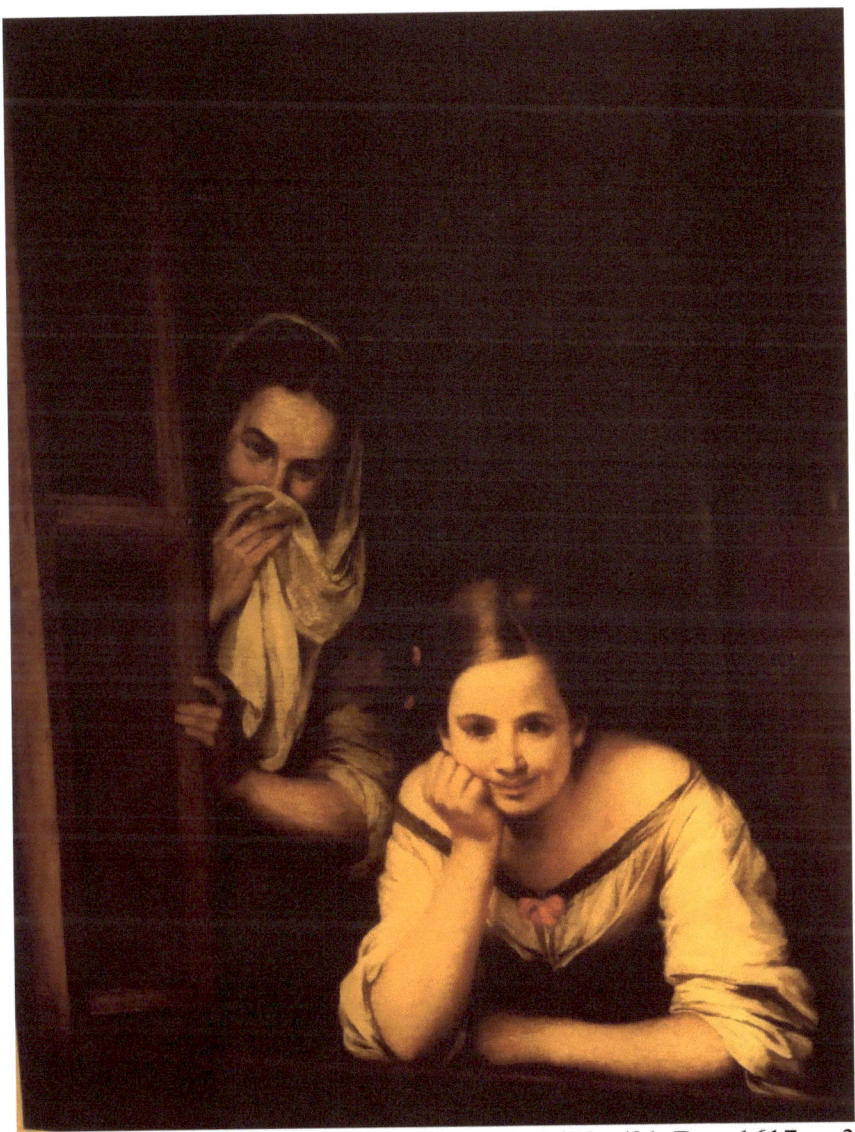

Bartolomé Esteban Murillo, 53, 1670, (31 Dec 1617 – 3 April 1682, aged 64.2, Spanish painter), A Girl and Her Duenna, at the National Gallery of Art in Washington, D.C.

1684 – Rembrandt's fifth child, an illegitimate daughter with Hendrickje Stoffels, Cornelia passed away at 30 (30 Oct 1654 – 1684).

1686 – Rembrandt's granddaughter Titia van Rijn, 17, (1669 – 1715, aged 46) married François van Bijler.

1715 – Rembrandt's granddaughter Titia van Rijn passed away at 46 (1669 – 1715).

1724 – "Treatise on Painting by Leonardo da Vinci" was published in Germany – contained Leonardo's work on the studies of anatomy, light and the landscape, which were assembled for publication by his pupil Francesco Melzi.

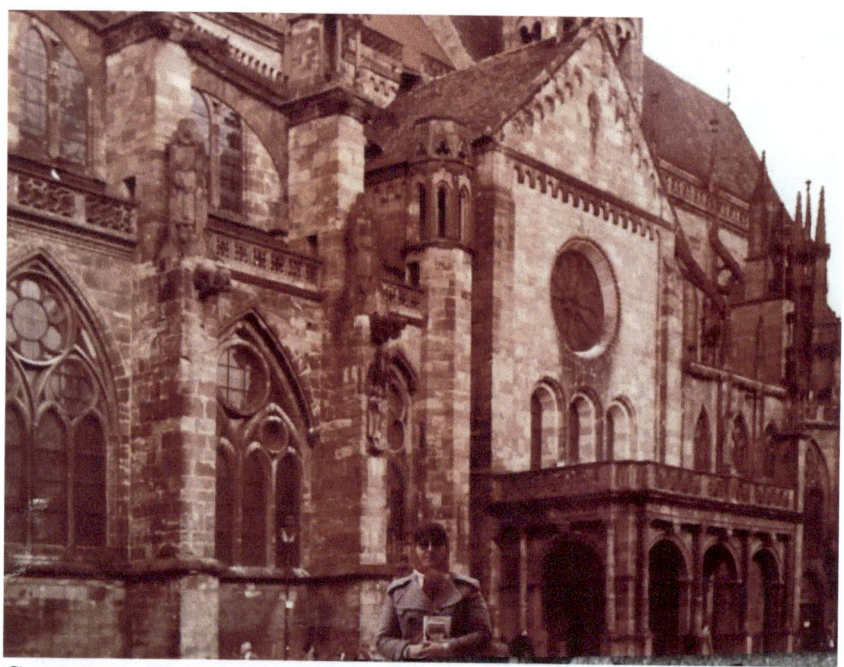

Germany - 23 March 1978, Freibourg im Breisgau (1120 by Duke Berthold III of Zähringen (1085-1122), elevation 278 m, the south façade of Freiburger Münster (cathedral, 1200, 116 m, J. S. Bach (1685-1750) performed here).

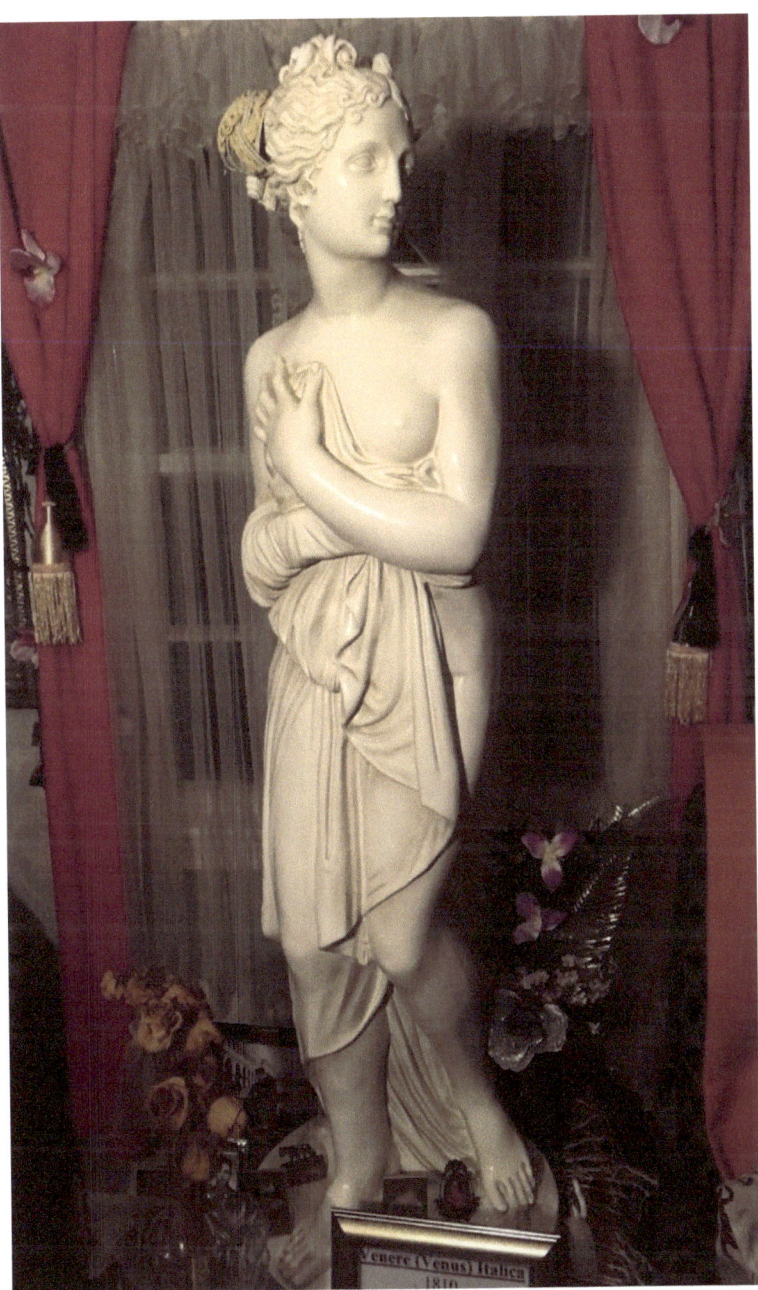

1810 – Antonio Canova (1757 – 1822, aged 65, sculptor from Venezia) finished Venere (Venus) Italica, a carved Carrara marble sculpture, 1.75 m, commissioned by Napoleon Bonaparte (1769 – 1821, aged 52).

Chapter 3. Auguste Rodin

1840 – 12 November - Birth of François Auguste René Rodin, known as Auguste Rodin in the Rue de l'Arbalète, in the 12th arrondissement (present 5th arrondissement), a working-class area of Paris. His father was Jean-Baptiste Rodin, 37, (1803 – 1883, aged 80, clerk in a police station, and then police inspector), and his mother Marie Rodin (circa 1806 – 1871, aged circa 65) August was the second child, after his sister Maria (1838 – 1862, aged 24).

14 November – two days after August Rodin, Claude Monet was born (14 Nov 1840 – 5 Dec 1926, aged 86 years and 3 weeks, French painter).

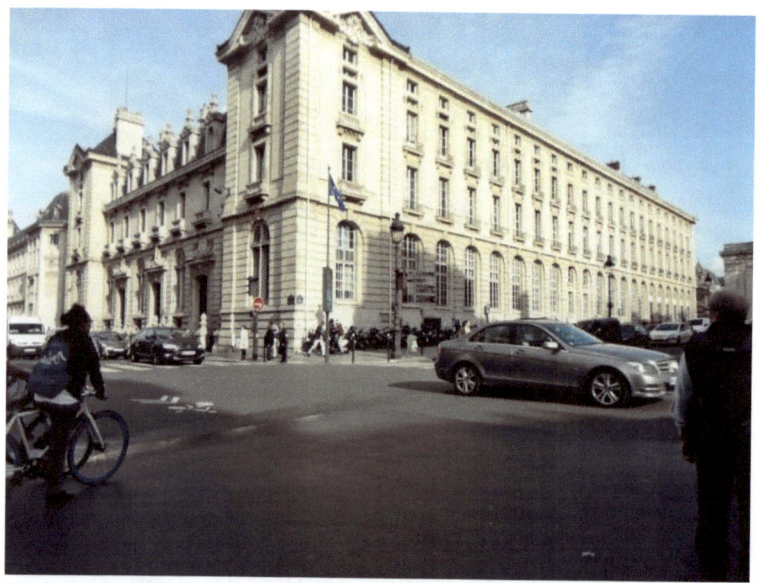

Université Paris 1 Panthéon-Sorbonne (1971, after the division of the University of Paris (Sorbonne, 1150)), on Rue Saint-Jacques (left) and Rue Soufflot (right, to Panthéon (1758 – 1790)), 1 km northwest from the Rue de l'Arbalète.

1841 – 28 September – August Rodin was 10.5 months old when Georges Clemenceau was born (28 Sep 1841 – 24 Nov 1929, aged 88.1, medical doctor and the 54th Prime Minister of France (25 Oct 1906 – 24 July 1909, and 16 Nov 1917 – 20 Jan 1920).

1850 – August Rodin, 10, was largely self-educated, and began to draw.
18 August - Honoré de Balzac passed away aged 51.2 (20 May 1799 – 18 August 1850, French novelist and playwright).

1854 – Rodin, 13.5, persuaded his father, who noticed his son's drawing talent, to let him attend the École Impériale Spéciale de Dessin et de Mathématiques – known as the "Petite École", a school specializing in art and mathematics– where his drawing teacher was the painter Horace Lecoq de Boisbaudran (14 May 1802 – 7 August 1897, aged 95.2, French artist and teacher), for 3 years, until 1857. These three years were essential for his training: while learning traditional techniques, he improved his powers of observation, and practiced drawing from memory. At this school Rodin met Jules Dalou, 15, (31 Dec 1838 – 15 April 1902, aged 63.3, French sculptor), and Alphonse Legros, 17, (8 May 1837 – 8 Dec 1911, aged 74.6, French painter, etcher, sculptor, and medalist).

1855 – Rodin, 14.5, received a bronze medal for drawing, joins the sculpture class, and spends much of his time sketching in the Louvre, in the print department of the Imperial Library, and at the Gobelins Tapestry Factory.

1856 – Rodin, 15.5, draws a copy after an antic scene, and a Nude Male.
13 May - Father Pierre-Julian Eymard, 45.2, (4 Feb 1811 – 1 August 1868, aged 57.5, French Catholic priest and founder of two religious institutes: the Congregation of the Blessed Sacrament for men and the Servants of the Blessed Sacrament for women) founded the order Congregation of the Blessed Sacrament.

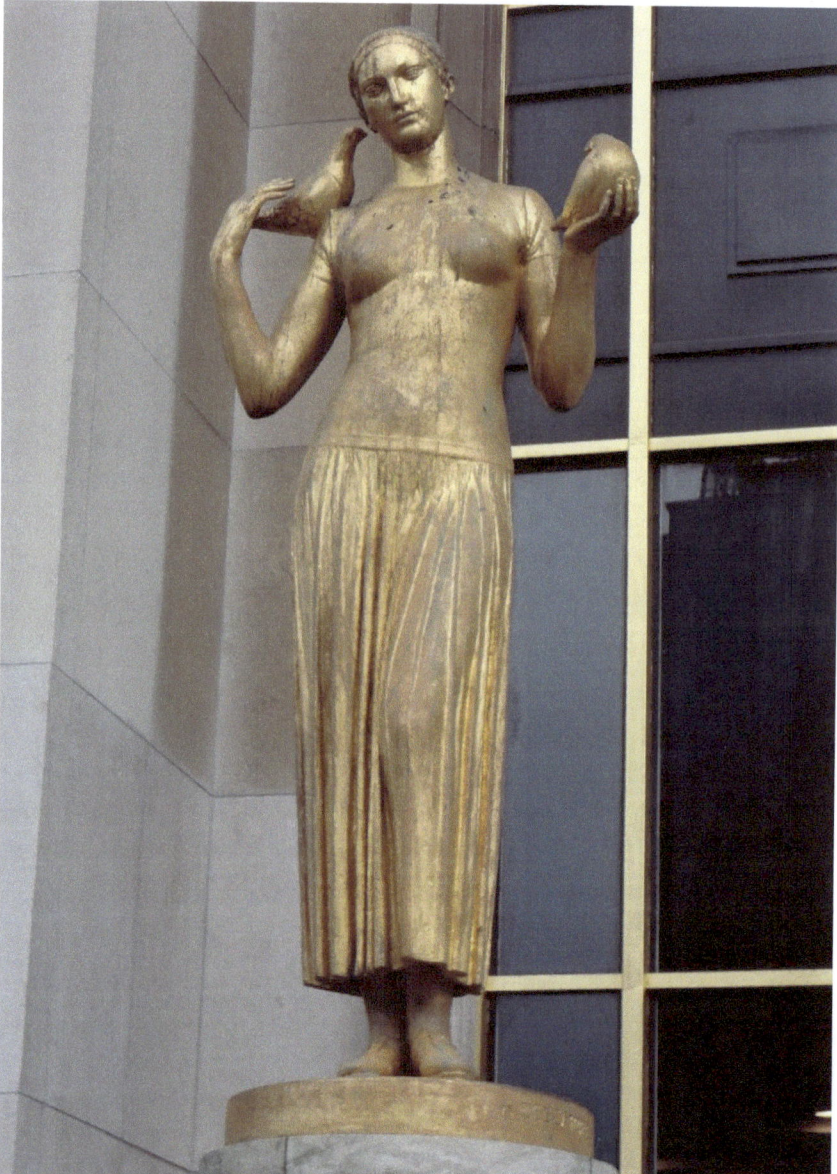

The statue "La Jeunesse" (1937) by Alexandre Descatoire (1874 – 1949, French sculptor, was a pupil of André-Louis-Adolphe Laoust (1843 – 1924), educated at the École nationale supérieure des Beaux-Arts in Paris, he was runner up for the Prix de Rome of 1902), on the south-west façade of Palais de Chaillot (1937, named after a former village which was here, with architectural, naval and ethnographic museums), on the hill of the Trocadéro.

1857 – Rodin, 16.5, received a top award for drawing, leaves the "Petite École", and applied (submitting a clay model of a companion) to the École des Beaux-Arts (also called Grande École) to study sculpture. He fails the entrance examination three times in a row. He thus commences his artistic career outside of official channels, and earned a living as a craftsman and ornamentor for most of the next two decades, producing decorative objects and architectural embellishments.

1858 – Rodin, 17.5, in order to assist his family financially, works with several decorative artists and ornamentalists.
He meets again the sculptor Jules Dalou, 19.

1860 – Rodin, 20, created his first sculpture: bust of Jean-Baptiste Rodin, 57, his father, portrayed as a Roman legislator.

1862 – Rodin was 22 when his sister Maria passed away of peritonitis (probably from tuberculosis) in a convent, aged 24.
Rodin was tormented with guilt, because he had introduced her to an unfaithful suitor. He turned away from art, and joined the Catholic order of the Congregation of the Blessed Sacrament as a novice, under the name Brother Augustin. Father Pierre-Julian Eymard, 51, founder and head of the congregation, recognized Rodin's talent, and sensed his lack of suitability for the order, so he encouraged Rodin to continue with his sculpture. Rodin returned to work as a decorator.

1863 – Rodin, 23, makes the bust Le Père Eymard, of Father Pierre-Julian Eymard, 52.

1864 – Rodin, 24, attended classes in animal anatomy run by animal sculptor Antoine Louis Barye, 69, (24 Sep 1795 – 25 June 1875, aged 79.7), at the Muséum National d'Histoire Naturelle, Paris.
He meets the young seamstress Rose Beuret, 20, (June 1844 – 16 Feb 1917, aged 72.6), who becomes his lifelong companion. She was one of Rodin's models, and her first portrait was named after Goethe's heroine, Mignon.

Rodin starts working with the sculptor Albert Ernest Carrier-Belleuse, 40, (1824-1896, aged 72), for whom he produces decorative works, most frequently signed by his employer. Rodin learns all the details of running a large studio. The most representative work from this period is Young Woman in a Floral Hat.

1865 – Rodin, 25, created The Man with the Broken Nose, which was rejected by the Salon jury. It reveals the battered face of a poor man of the neighborhood named "Bibi". But a particularly harsh winter (1864 – 1865) froze the head made of raw clay, which split to the point that the back part broke. Reduced to a mask, this work was considered incomplete.

1866 – 18 January – Rodin, 25.2, and his unofficial wife Rose Beuret, 21.5, had a son, Auguste-Eugène Beuret (18 Jan 1866 – 1934, aged 68, future draughtsman and engraver).
Rodin entered the studio of Albert-Ernest Carrier-Belleuse, 42, (12 June 1824 – 4 June 1887, aged 62.9, French sculptor, he did en equestrian statue of Mihai Viteazul in Bucharest, Romania), a successful mass producer of objects d'art. Rodin worked as Carrier-Belleuse' chief assistant for 4 years, until 1870, designing roof decorations and staircase and doorway embellishments. Rodin did a bust of Carrier-Belleuse.

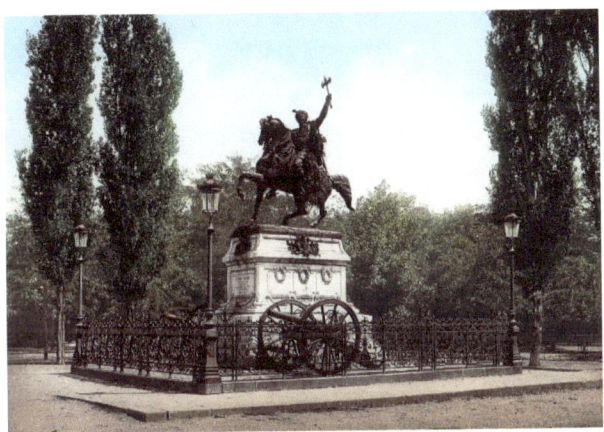

Equestrian statue of Mihai Viteazul in Bucharest, Romania, by Albert-Ernest Carrier-Belleuse (12 June 1824 – 4 June 1887, aged 62.9, French sculptor who worked with August Rodin.

1867 – Rodin was 27 when Claude Monet, 27 (two days younger than Rodin) finished the painting Saint Germain l'Auxerrois and Women in the Garden.

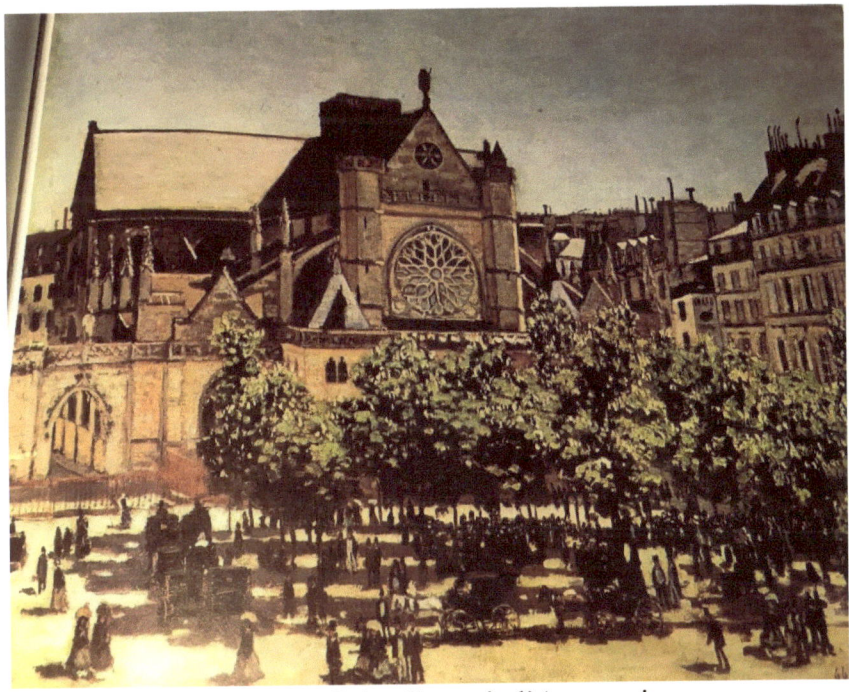

Claude Monet, 27, 1867, Saint Germain l'Auxerrois

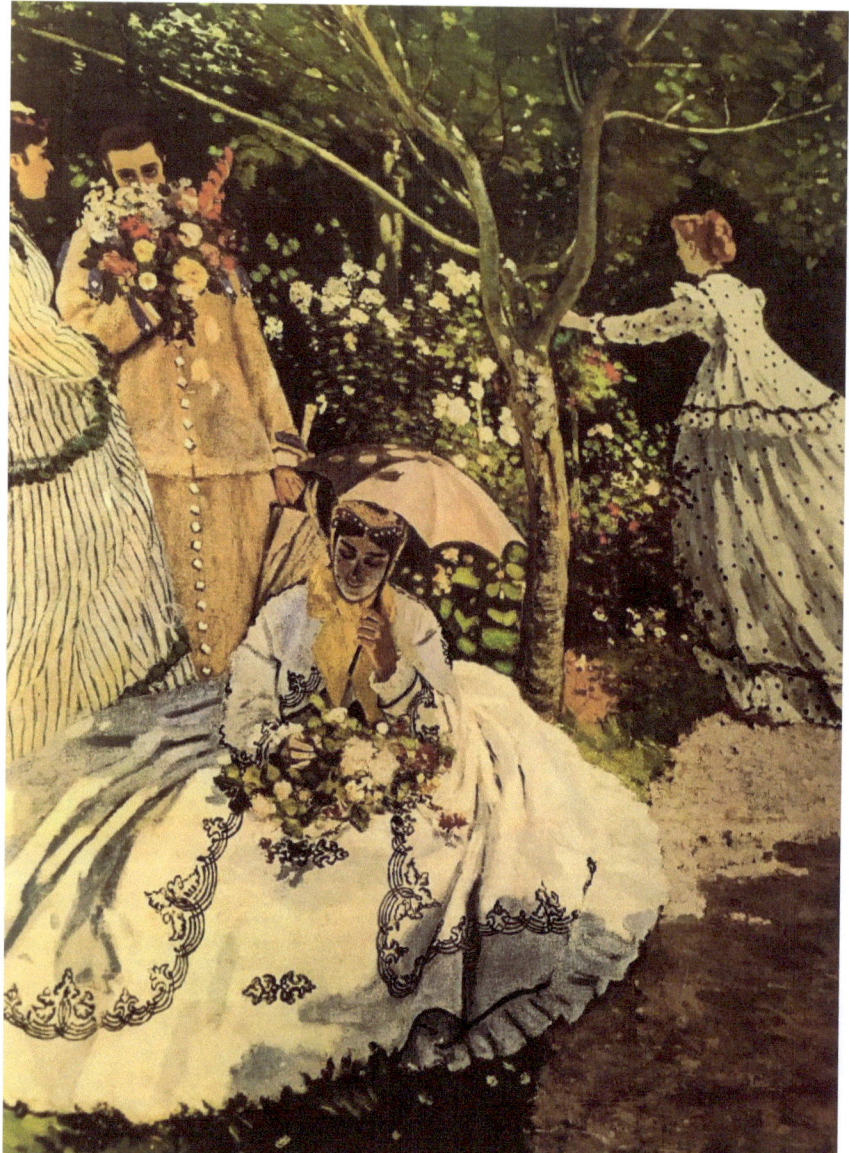

Claude Monet, 27 (two days younger than Rodin), 1867, Women in the Garden

1870 – Rodin, 29.5, was drafted into a regiment of the Garde Nationale, because of the Franco-Prussian War, and was given his corporal's stripes, but he was soon discharged on the grounds of nearsightedness.

Rodin, with his son Auguste-Eugène being 4 years old, draws Three nude children.

1871 – Rodin, 31, joins Albert Ernest Carrier-Belleuse, 47, in Belgium, and worked on ornamentation for the Brussels Stock Exchange, and on various decorative schemes on buildings and monuments.
Rodin's mother, Marie Rodin, passed away aged circa 65.
Rodin takes part in an exhibition for the first time in Belgium.

1872 – Rodin, 32, ended his collaboration with Albert Ernest Carrier-Belleuse, 48, because Carrier-Belleuse discovered that Rodin shows his works under his own name.
Rose Beuret, 28, joins Rodin in Brussels.

1873 – Rodin, 33, signed a contract with the Belgian sculptor Antoine-Joseph Van Rasbourgh, 42, (1831 - 1902, aged 71), who was also a Carrier-Belleuse's former employee. Their main source of income comes from the decoration of public buildings in Brussels. Rodin executes the Atalantes and Caryatids on the Boulevard Anspach, in an independent manner. He submits entries to the International Exhibitions in London and Vienna.

1874 – Rodin, 34, works on the decoration of the Palais des Académies, Brussels.
He executes a series of landscapes in the forest of Soignes (Dirt Track to Watermael through the Forest of Soignes, Golden Twilight on the Dunes in the Forest of Soignes, A clearing spot in the forest of Soignes, between 1871 and 1877, where Rodin enjoys walking with Rose), including about thirty small landscape paintings, mounted on cardboard, and ten red chalk drawings.
He produces lithographs used as illustrations in the satirical magazine Le Petit Comique.
Claude Monet, 34, painted The Boats Regatta at Argenteuil.

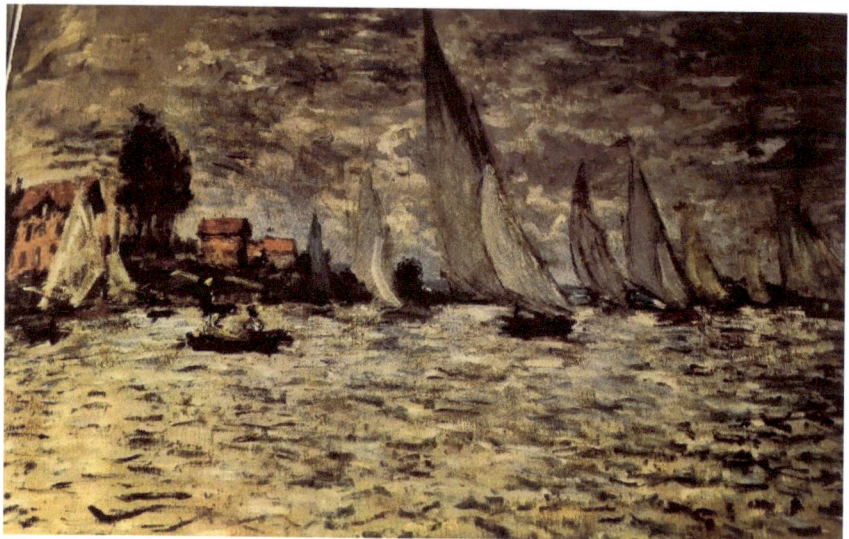

Claude Monet, 34, 1874, The Boats Regatta at Argenteuil

1875 – 1 May - Rodin, 34.5, exhibits Man with the Broken Nose at the Paris Salon, until 20 June. He is very fond of this sculpture, which he regards as his "first good sculpture". The acceptance of his work at the Salon is a victory in itself, even if the general public have not yet heard of the sculptor Rodin.

He travels to Italy for two months to study the works of Renaissance artists, especially Michelangelo. As soon as Rodin returned to Belgium, he designed a life-size nude study as a tribute to the Florentine sculptor. Initially shown without a title, then called, in turn, The Vanquished One and The Awakening Man, it is eventually named The Age of Bronze, an allusion to the third of the four ages of mankind, as described by the early Greek poet Hesiod. The sculpture drew inspiration from Michelangelo's Dying Slave, which Rodin had observed at the Louvre.

1876 – Rodin was 36 when his works are shown at the Centennial International Exhibition, in Philadelphia, USA.

19 February – a future student of Rodin, Constantin Brâncuși, was born (19 Feb 1876, Hobița, Gorj, Romania – 16 March 1957, Paris, France, aged 81 years and 25 days, Romanian sculptor, painter and photographer who made his career in France).

Pierre-Auguste Renoir, known as Auguste Renoir, 35, (25 February 1841 – 3 December 1919, aged 78.8, French painter) painted Girl with Sheaf of Corn.

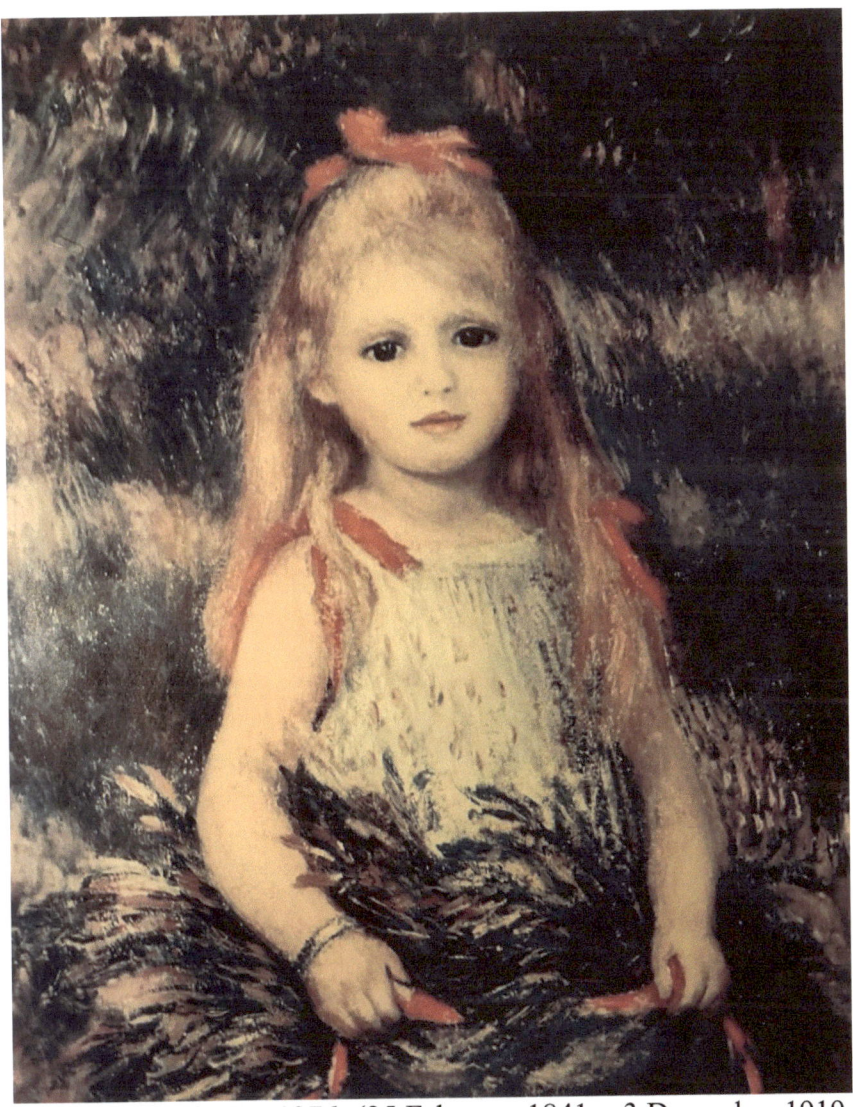

Auguste Renoir, 35, 1876, (25 February 1841 – 3 December 1919, aged 78.8, French painter), Girl with Sheaf of Corn.

1877 – Rodin, 37, after spending over six years in Belgium, returned to Paris, and exhibited L'age d'airain (The Age of Bronze) at the Salon des Artistes Français, Paris, after it debuted in Brussels earlier.

Rodin and Rose, 33, moved into a small flat on La Rive Gauche (Left Bank of River Seine). His father, 74, was blind and senile, cared for by Rodin's sister-in-law, Aunt Thérèse. Rodin's son Auguste, 11, possibly developmentally delayed, was also in Thérèse's care.

He completes the model for the Monument to Byron, which he submits to the competition in London.

Autumn - Rodin embarks upon his first tour of French cathedrals in the center of France.

He begins working as an ornamental sculptor again, due to financial hardship. He makes notably mascarons (Fine Weather and Bad Weather) decorating the fountain at the Palais du Trocadéro, built for the Paris Exposition Universelle of 1878.

Rodin earned his living collaborating with more established sculptors on public commissions, primarily memorials and neo-baroque architectural pieces. In competitions for commissions he submitted models of Denis Diderot (5 Oct 1713 – 31 July 1784, aged 70.8, French philosopher and write), Jean-Jacques Rousseau (28 June 1712 – 2 July 1778, aged 66 years and 4 days, Genevan philosopher, writer and composer), and Lazare Carnot (13 May 1753 – 2 August 1823, aged 70.2, French mathematician, physicist and politician), but without success. On his own time, he worked on studies leading to the creation of his next important work, St. John the Baptist Preaching - the model was an Italian peasant who presented himself at Rodin's studio.

1878 – Rodin, 38, created L'homme qui marche (The Walking Man), and completed St. John the Baptist Preaching (2 m).

1879 – Rodin, 39, worked in Marseilles on the decoration of the Palais des Beaux-Arts, and in Nice on the decoration of the Villa Neptune.

He makes vases, adorned with hollow-cut and relief motifs, in a variety of shapes and colors, for the Sèvres Porcelain Factory (run by Carrier-Belleuse), from 1879 to 1882.

1880 – Rodin, 40, received an offer from Carrier-Belleuse, 56, – now art director of the Sèvres national porcelain factory – for a part-time position as a designer, and he accepted. Rodin immersed himself in designs for vases and table ornaments that brought the factory renown across Europe.
He begins to frequent artistic and literary circles, notably the salon of Madame Edmond Adam, 44, (4 Oct 1836 - 23 August 1936, aged 99 years 10 months and 19 days), the wife of Edmond Adam (19 Nov 1816 – 14 June 1877, aged 60.6, French politician and superior official) for 9 years, between 1868 (he was 52, she was 32) and 1877 (she was widow at 40.6), a woman of letters who founded La Nouvelle Revue last year, in 1879. At this salon Rodin met prominent French stateman Leon Gambetta, 42, (2 April 1838 – 31 Dec 1882, aged 44.7, the 37th Prime Minister of France for 2.5 months (14 Nov 1881 – 30 Jan 1882 (death)). Rodin impressed Gambetta, who spoke of Rodin in turn to several government ministers, including Edmund Turquet, 44, (31 May 1836 – 8 Feb 1914, aged 77.7, the Undersecretary of the Ministry of Fine Arts), whom Rodin eventually met. Through him, he won the 1880 commission to create a portal for a planned museum of decorative arts. Rodin dedicated much of the next 35 years to his elaborate Gates of Hell (a monumental sculptural group depicting scenes from Dante's Inferno in high relief), an unfinished portal for a museum that was never built. Many of the portal's figures became sculptures in themselves, including Rodin's most famous, The Thinker and The Kiss. With the museum commission came a free studio. Soon, he stopped working at the porcelain factory; his income came from private commissions.
   Rodin was invited to Paris Salons by such friends as writer Léon Cladel, 46, (22 March 1834 – 21 July 1892, aged 58.3, French novelist).
   He moved into his first studio at the Dépôt des Marbres, 182, rue de l'Université (1.5 km southeast of L'Arc de Triomphe, and 1.3 km southwest of Place de la Concorde), which he would keep for the rest of his life.

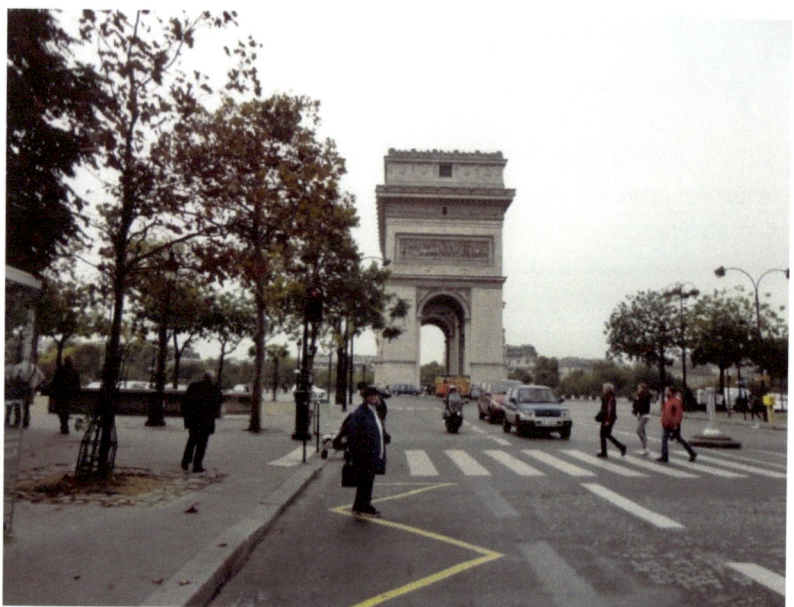

The north side of l'Arc de Triomphe de l'Étoile, started by Napoleon in 1806, height 50 m, wide 45 m, deep 22 m, in the center of the Place Charles de Gaulle, from Av. de Wagram.

Thanks to recommendations made by Rodin's friends, the French government purchases a cast of The Age of Bronze for the sum of 2,000 francs (what it had cost Rodin to have it cast in bronze, about $10,000, which was the salary of a worker in 1880 for 4 years).

Rodin submitted the sculpture St. John the Baptist Preaching to the Paris Salon, and the piece finished third in the Salon's sculpture category.

Inspired by Dante's Divine Comedy, Rodin would work on The Gates of Hell project for the rest of his life, without ever delivering it, or seeing it cast in bronze. Well-known works derived from The Gates are The Three Shades, Ugolino, Fallen Caryatid Carrying her Stone, Fugit Amor, She Who Was Once the Helmet-Maker's Beautiful Wife, The Falling Man, and The Prodigal Son. The Gates would remain a repertory of figures – constantly reworked, rearranged and modified – which Rodin gradually built up, and was to draw on throughout his career (the unfinished Gates of Hell, with 186 figures, is now at Kunsthaus, Zürich, Switzerland).

1881 – Rodin was 41 when the French government purchased a bronze cast of Saint John the Baptist Preaching.

His first visit to England took place, during which the etcher Alphonse Legros introduces him to engraving. On his advice, Rodin tried his hand at several dry-point etchings.

Rodin models the figures of Adam (plaster), Ève (bronze) and The Thinker (originally titled The Poet, after Dante, 70 cm high, bronze, created between 1879 and 1889).

1882 – Rodin, 42, designed a sculptural group depicting a couple entwined in each other's arms, their lips joined in a kiss, to be fitted onto the lower left door of The Gates of Hell. Subsequently called The Kiss, the work would remain on The Gates until 1886.

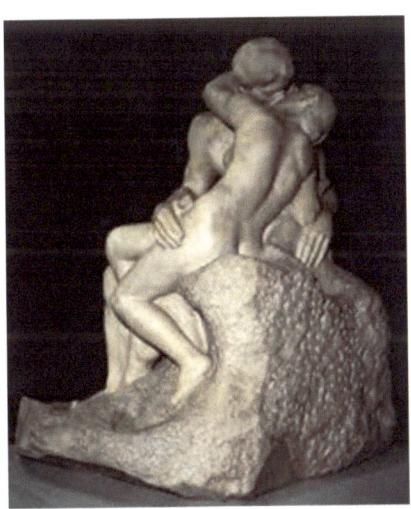

The Kiss

1883 – Rodin, 43, makes the Bust of Jules Dalou, 45, in order to celebrate the medal of honor that Dalou obtained in the Salon.

Rodin agreed to supervise a course for sculptor Alfred Boucher, 33, (23 Sep 1850 – 1934, aged 84) in his absence, where he met Camille Claudel 18.5, (8 Dec 1864 – 19 Oct 1943, aged 78.8), who became his new pupil. The two formed a passionate relationship, and Claudel inspired Rodin as a model for many of his figures.

His father, Jean-Baptiste Rodin, passed away aged 80.

1884 – Rodin, 44, makes a bust of Camille Claudel, 20.

1885 – Rodin, 45, received a commission from the city of Calais for a monument to commemorate Eustache de Saint Pierre, the eldest of the six towns' men of Calais who offered their lives to save their fellow citizens, which would become the Monument to The Burghers of Calais.

22 May - Victor Hugo died, aged 83.2 (26 Feb 1802 – 22 May 1885, French poet, novelist, and dramatist).

1886 – Rodin, 46, received a commission from the city of Santiago, Chile, for Monuments to Benjamin Vicuña Mackenna and General Lynch.

1887 – Rodin, 47, illustrated Paul Gallimard's copy of The Flowers of Evil by Charles Baudelaire.

1888 – Rodin, 48, received a commission from The French government for a marble version of The Kiss, for the Paris Exposition Universelle of 1889.

He is photographed in his studio, leaning on his sculpture The Kiss.

1889 – Rodin, 49, was one of the founder members of the Société Nationale des Beaux-Arts.

The Paris Salon invited Rodin to be a judge on its artistic jury.

He created Les Bourgeois de Calais (The Burghers of Calais), and The Kiss.

Les Bourgeois de Calais (The Burghers of Calais) was first displayed to general acclaim. It is a bronze sculpture weighing (1,814 kg), and its figures are 2 m tall.

"Claude Monet – Auguste Rodin" exhibition was held at the Galerie Georges Petit.

Rodin received a commission for the Monument to Claude Lorrain, unveiled in Nancy in 1892.

He also received a commission for the Monument to Victor Hugo (26 Feb 1802 – 22 May 1885, aged 83.2, French poet, novelist, and dramatist) to be erected at the Panthéon, Paris.

There is a statue of Victor Hugo in Rome, Italy. It is across from the Museo Carlo Bilotti on Viale Fiorello La Guardia.

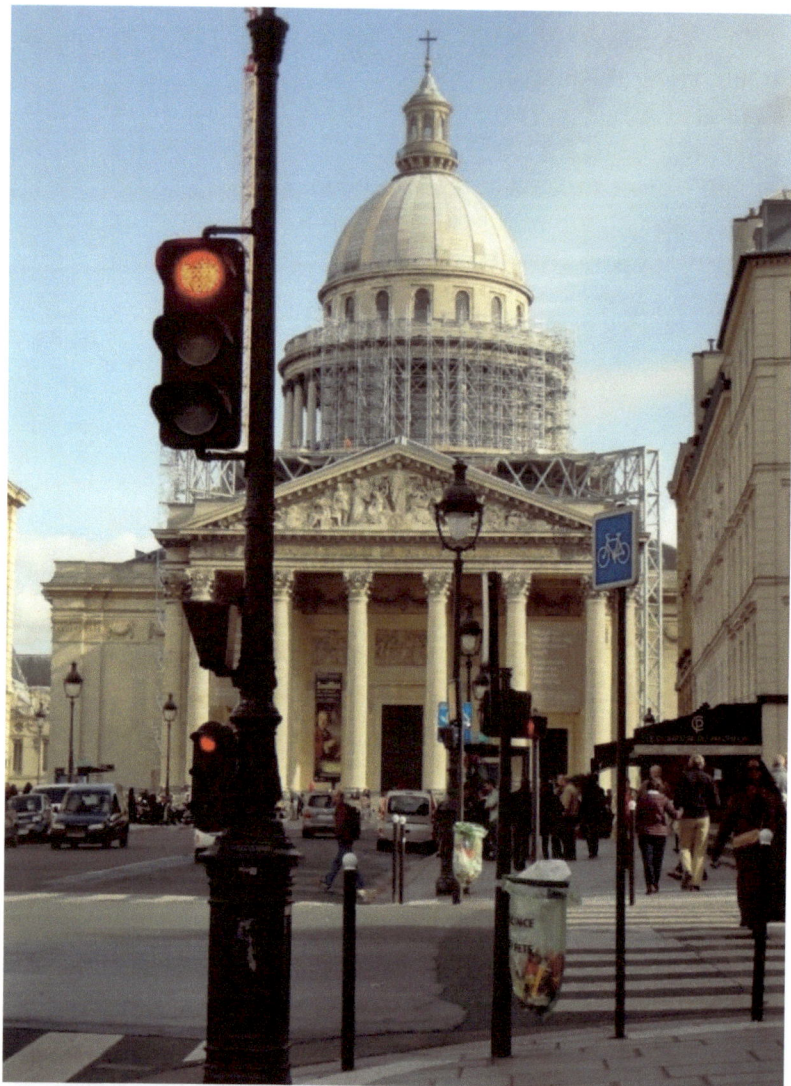

The Panthéon (1758 - 1790, 83 m height, mausoleum in the Latin Quarter in Paris, modeled on the Pantheon in Rome), seen from Rue Soufflot, near Rue Saint-Jacques. This mausoleum, with the motto: *Aux grands hommes, la patrie reconnaissante* ("To the great men, the grateful homeland"), contains the remains of distinguished French citizens (Voltaire, Rousseau, Victor Hugo, etc.). In 1851, physicist Léon Foucault demonstrated the rotation of the earth by his experiment conducted in the Panthéon, by constructing a 67 m Foucault pendulum beneath the central dome.

1890 – Rodin was 50 when his Monument to Victor Hugo was not favorably received.

1891 – Rodin, 51, worked on a new model for the Monument to Victor Hugo, for the Panthéon, Paris; a cast of his initial project is commissioned for a public park.
The Société des Gens de Lettres commissions him to design a Monument to Honoré de Balzac.

1892 – Rodin was 52 when his Monument to Claude Lorrain was unveiled in Nancy.
He created a Bust of Balzac, which is now displayed at the Victoria and Albert Museum.
Camille Claudel, 28, created a bust of Rodin.

1893 – Rodin, 53, succeeded Dalou as vice-president of the Société Nationale des Beaux-Arts, and president of the sculpture section.
He employs the sculptor Antoine Bourdelle as his studio assistant. His students included Antoine Bourdelle, 32, (30 Oct 1861 – 1 Oct 1929, aged 67.9, French sculptor, painter and teacher), and Charles Despiau, 19, (4 Nov 1874 – 30 Oct 1946, aged 71.9, French sculptor).
Rodin rented the Villa des Brillants, in Meudon.

1894 – Rodin, 54, was invited to Claude Monet's home in Giverny, where he meets Paul Cézanne.
Rodin was commissioned for the Monument to Sarmiento, to be erected in Buenos Aires (Argentina), and unveiled in 1900.

1895 – Rodin, 55, purchased the Villa des Brillants, in Meudon (8 km southwest of L'Arc de Triomphe), which he has rented since 1893. In Meudon, he is, however, still within close proximity of his studios, to which he can commute by train or boat.
Rodin started to build up his collection of antiques and paintings. He soon assembles a large number of objects from different civilizations and areas, purchased through dealers, at public sales or from private collectors.

Unveiling of the Monument to the Burghers of Calais, in Calais. The work was placed in front of a public garden on a high platform, surrounded by a cast-iron railing. Rodin had wanted it located near the town hall, where it would engage the public. Only after damage during the First World War, subsequent storage, and Rodin's death, was the sculpture displayed as he had intended.

1896 – Rodin was 56 when "Rodin, Puvis de Chavannes, Carrière" exhibition opened at the Musée Rath, in Geneva, Switzerland.

Rodin was photographed observing work on the monument to Victor Hugo at the studio (26 rue du Chemin-Vert in Paris, 2 km northeast of the Cathédrale Notre Dame de Paris) of his assistant Henri Lebossé.

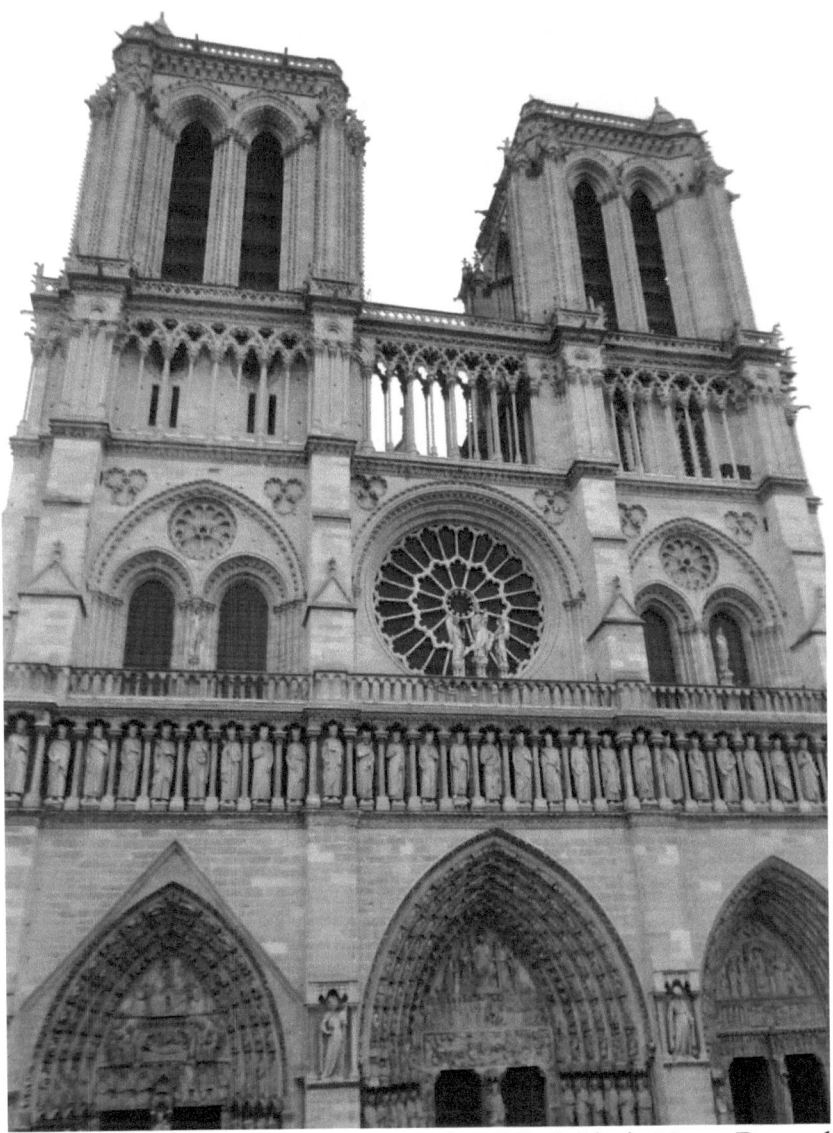

The upper part of the western façade of Cathédrale Notre Dame de Paris (1163 – 1345, 90 m), on the south-eastern part of the Île de la Cité, which is considered the center of Paris, in the fourth arrondissement. The organ has 7,374 pipes, with about 900 classified as historical. It has 110 real stops, five 56-key manuals and a 32-key pedalboard; it is now fully computerized. The Towers at Notre-Dame contain five church bells. The great bourdon bell, Emmanuel, from 1681, 13 t, is located in the South Tower (right).

1897 – Rodin was 57 when Maurice Fenaille, one of his patrons, finances the publication of a volume of 142 drawings by Rodin, with a preface by Octave Mirbeau, known as the "Goupil Album" (named after the publisher).

His plaster model of the Monument to Victor Hugo was shown at the Société Nationale des Beaux-Arts, and it was cast in bronze 67 years later, in 1964.

1898 – Rodin, 58, ended his 15 years of relationship with Camille Claudel, 34, permanently. Claudel suffered a nervous breakdown 15 years later, in 1913, at 49, and was confined to an institution for almost 30 years by her family, until her death on 19 Oct 1943.

The Société des Gens de Lettres did not have a favorable view of his plaster of Honoré de Balzac (20 May 1799 – 18 August 1850, age 51.2, French novelist and playwright), shown at the Salon de la Société Nationale des Beaux-Arts. Rodin repaid the Société des Gens de Lettres his commission, and moved the statue to his garden. A manifesto defending him was signed by Claude Monet, 58 (two days younger than Rodin), (14 Nov 1840 – 5 Dec 1926, aged 86 years and 3 weeks, French painter), Claude Debussy, 36, (22 August 1862 – 25 March 1918, aged 55.6, French composer), and future Premier Georges Clemenceau, 57, (28 Sep 1841 – 24 Nov 1929, aged 88.1, medical doctor and 54th Prime Minister of France (25 Oct 1906 – 24 July 1909, and 16 Nov 1917 – 20 Jan 1920)), among many others. Now a cast of the Monument to Balzac is exposed in Jardin du Musée Rodin, and the same statue was cast in bronze after 41 years, in 1939, and placed on the Boulevard du Montparnasse at the intersection with Boulevard Raspail (1 km southwest of Palais de Luxembourg, and 1.1 km west of L'École Normale Supérieure in Paris).

1899 – Rodin, 59, received the commission for the Monument to Pierre Puvis de Chavannes.

His first solo exhibition opens in Brussels (Belgium), then Rotterdam, Amsterdam and The Hague (the Netherlands).

His large bronze Ève is shown at the Salon de la Société Nationale des Beaux-Arts.

1900 – Rodin, 60, was appointed Knight of the Order of Leopold of Belgium.

To coincide with the Exposition Universelle, he decided to organize his first solo exhibition in France, in a pavilion specially built for the occasion on the Place de l'Alma, Paris. Almost one and a half month after the official opening of the Exposition Universelle, Rodin inaugurated his own exhibition: many artists, politicians, connoisseurs and collectors, from several countries, attended the lesson of the sculptor.

His Monument to Sarmiento, was erected in Buenos Aires, Argentina, and unveiled.

Rodin was photographed in front of his studio at the Dépôt des Marbres, on the courtyard side, and in the pavilion on the Place de l'Alma.

1901 – Rodin was 61 when his Pavilion is dismantled and reconstructed on the grounds of the Villa des Brillants, in Meudon. It is converted into a studio.

A major exhibition of Eugène Druet's photographs of Rodin's works is held at the Galerie des Artistes Modernes.

1902 – Rodin was 62 when he created Le Penseur (The Thinker).

A major "Rodin" exhibition opened in Prague.

The sculptor meets the poet Rainer Maria Rilke, 27, (1875 – 1926, aged 51), whom he employs as a secretary from 15 September 1905 to 12 May 1906.

Rodin illustrates the second edition of Octave Mirbeau's Le Jardin des supplices. The lithographs are printed by Auguste Clot, 44, (1858 – 1936, aged 78).

1903 – Rodin, 63, is named Commander of the Legion of Honor. To celebrate his decoration, Bourdelle organized a banquet in his honor in the Bois de Vélizy.

His international reputation attracts a new affluent celebrity clientele, who soon commission works from him. Wealthy society women flock to his studio to sit for their portrait busts. Because of its refinement and elegance, Rodin often prefers to use marble for his portraits of women.

1904 – Rodin, 64, became friend with Duchesse de Choiseul, from whom he would separate after 8 years, in 1912.

His first exhibition of The Thinker (large-scale plaster version) opened at the International Society of Painters, Sculptors and Gravers, London, then at the Paris Salon (bronze version).

Rodin had a liaison with Gwendolen Mary John, 28, (1876 – 1939, aged 63), a Welsh painter and woman of letters, who posed for the figure of the Muse in the Monument to Whistler.

Rodin takes part in the International Art Exhibition in Düsseldorf, Germany.

1905 – Rodin, 64.5, was appointed member of the Conseil Supérieur des Beaux-Arts. The University of Jena awards him an honorary doctorate.

He made a bust of the English politician George Wyndham, 42, (29 August 1863 – 8 June 1913, aged 49.8, Under-Secretary of State for War, and Chief Secretary for Ireland, Rector of two Universities – Glasgow and Edinburgh).

15 September - Rodin, 64.8, employs the poet Rainer Maria Rilke, 30, (1875 – 1926, aged 51) as a secretary for almost 8 months, until 12 May 1906.

Rodin invited in his workshop the young sculptor Constantin Brâncuși, 29, (19 Feb 1876, Hobița, Gorj, Romania – 16 March 1957, Paris, France, aged 81 years and 25 days, Romanian sculptor, painter and photographer who made his career in France). Brâncuși admired Rodin, but he left Rodin's studio after only two months, saying, "Nothing can grow under big trees".

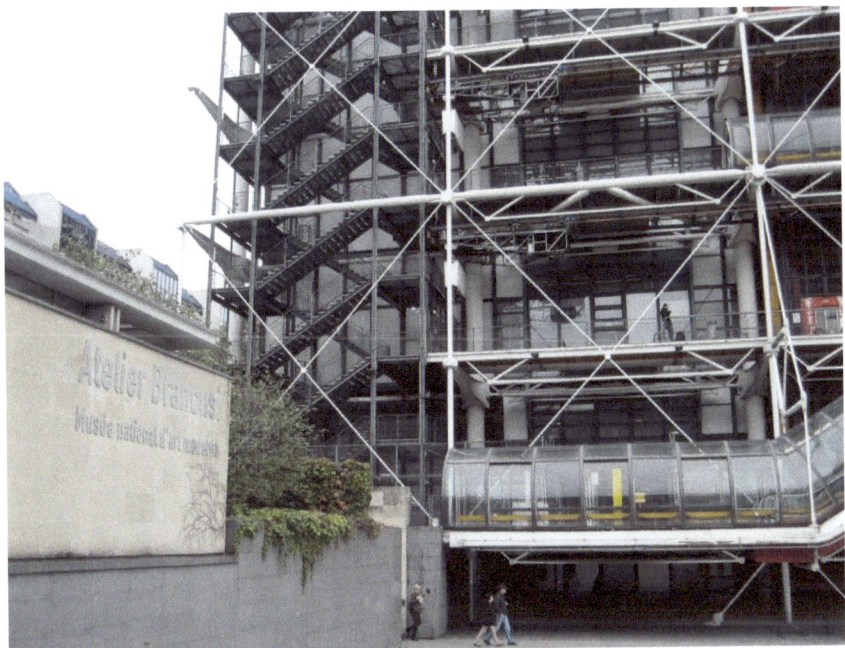

Paris: left: Atelier Brancusi (Constantin Brancusi, sculptor, 1876 – 1957), Musée national d'art moderne, on Rue Rambuteau; right: Centre Georges Pompidou (1971–1977, in the Beaubourg area).

1906 – Rodin, 66, was awarded a honorary doctorate from the University of Glasgow (where George Wyndham was the Rector), and appointed member of the Academy of Arts, Berlin.

His sculpture The Thinker was erected outside the Panthéon.

He made a bust of the Irish playwright George Bernard Shaw, 50, (26 July 1856 – 2 Nov 1950, aged 94.3).

Rodin painted a series of watercolors of Cambodian dancers, having seen them perform in Paris, then at the Colonial Exhibition in Marseille.

He meets the Japanese dancer Hanako, 38, (1868 – 1945, aged 77), who first poses for him, next year, in 1907.

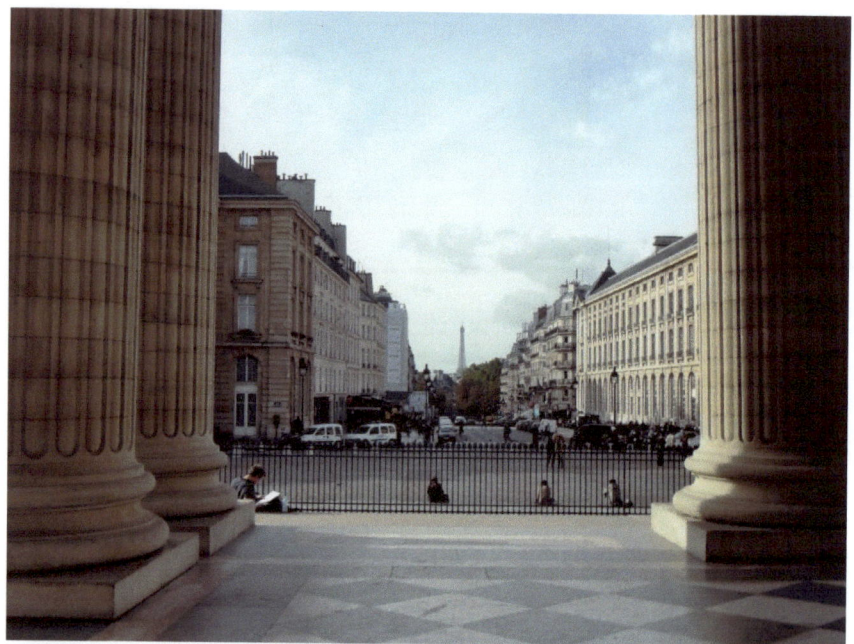

Mairie du V^m Arrondissement (left), Rue Soufflot (center, looking from Panthéon to Jardin du Luxembourg (1612) and Tour Eiffel (1889, 324 m)), with Université Paris 1 Panthéon-Sorbonne (right).

1907 – Rodin was 67 when Oxford University awarded him an honorary doctorate.

His first exhibition of only his drawings opened at the Galerie Bernheim-Jeune, Paris.

His sculpture Walking Man (large plaster) was shown at the Salon de la Société Nationale des Beaux-Arts.

1908 – Rodin, 68, models The Ark of the Covenant, later entitled The Cathedral.

He made a bust of the former mistress of the Prince of Wales who became King Edward VII, 67, (9 Nov 1841 – 6 May 1910, aged 68.5, King 22 Jan 1901 – 6 May 1910; King Edward visited Rodin in Meudon), Countess of Warwick, 47, (10 Dec 1861 – 26 July 1938, aged 76.6, married in 1881 (she was 20) Francis Greville, 5th Earl of Warwick, and had 5 children).

Rainer Maria Rilke, 33, tells him about the Hôtel Biron (1727 – 1732, rue de Varenne, 240 m east of Tombeau de Napoléon Ier). Threatened with demolition, this neglected former 18th-century mansion, flanked by buildings that have since been demolished, was in the hands of the receiver, and temporarily leased to various artists and writers for a very low rent. The sculptor decided to move in. He used the premises to receive admirers, journalists, art dealers and collectors, rather than as a workplace. In the garden, which was abandoned, Rodin scattered some antique sculptures from his collection.

Major exhibitions of Rodin's drawings opened in Vienna, Leipzig and Paris.

1909 – Rodin was 69 when the French government announces its decision to sell the Hôtel Biron estate. Rodin worked hard to save the mansion, and starts negotiating with the state.

He made a bust of the Austrian composer Gustav Mahler, 49, (7 July 1860 – 18 May 1911, aged 50.8).

An initial project for the Rodin Donation to the French nation appears, drawn up by the lawyer and politician Paul Escudier, 51, (1858 – 1931, aged 73), who supports Rodin's initiative.

Large exhibition of Rodin's drawings opened at the Galerie Devambez, Paris.

1910 – Rodin, 70, was named Grand Officier of the Legion of Honor.

He mentored the Russian sculptor, Moissey Kogan, 31, (12 March 1879 – 3 March 1943, aged 63.9).

Exhibition of his drawings opened in the meeting room of the periodical Gil Blas, in Paris.

He was photographed in front of his collection of antiques.

1911 – Rodin was 71 when his exhibition at the Prussian Academy of Arts in Berlin opened.

He made a bust of Georges Clemenceau, 70.

The French government commissioned him for the Bust of Pierre Puvis de Chavannes, for the Panthéon.

His sculptures The Burghers of Calais were purchased by England and installed in the gardens of Westminster.

His sculpture Walking Man is erected in the courtyard of the Palazzo Farnese, Rome.

Publication of Art: Conversations with Paul Gsell, 41, (1870-1947, aged 77), a journalist, man of letters and art critic.

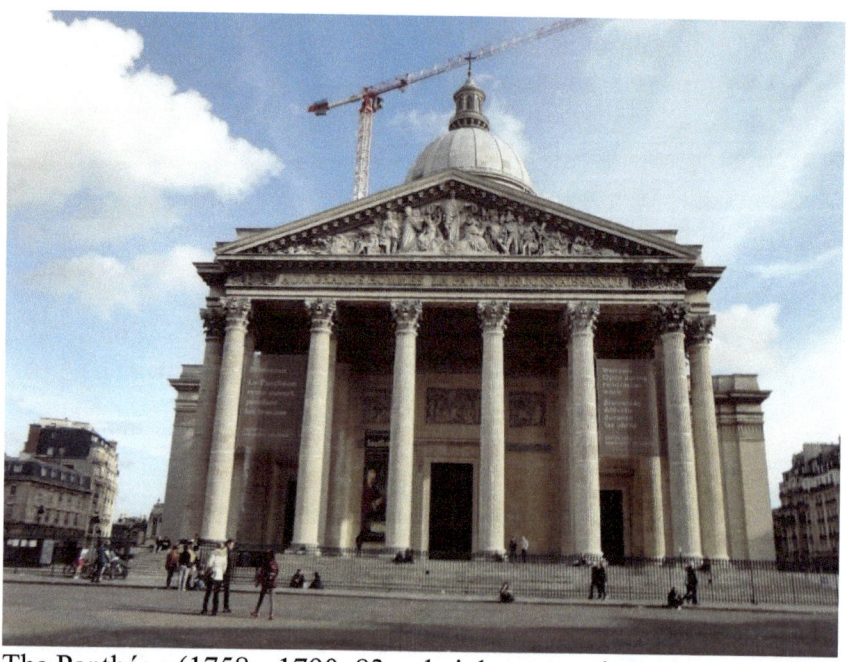

The Panthéon (1758 - 1790, 83 m height, mausoleum in the Latin Quarter in Paris, modeled on the Pantheon (126 AD) in Rome), seen from Rue Soufflot.

1912 – Rodin was 72 when "Rodin" exhibition opened in Tokyo, Japan.

Exhibition of Rodin's drawings at the new public library in Lyon, France, opened.

Inauguration of the Rodin Room at the Metropolitan Museum of New York takes place.

1913 – Rodin was 73 when his Exhibition at the Faculté de Médecine, Paris, where antiques from his collection appear for the first time, opened.

Rodin traveled to London to see the installation of The Burghers of Calais outside the Houses of Parliament.

1914 – Rodin, 74, compiled his notes full of descriptions of Gothic churches, jotted down on his travels all through his life, and published his book Les Cathédrales de France, illustrated with 100 reproductions of his drawings, printed by the lithographer Auguste Clot, with a preface by Charles Morice, 54, (1860 – 1919, aged 59). Fleeing the war, Rodin heads for England with Rose and Judith Cladel, then moves on to Rome, where he enjoys a gracious lifestyle, and takes immense pleasure in rediscovering the city's beauty. He spends almost all his time drawing.

December - Rodin was photographed at John Marshall's home in Rome.

1915 – Rodin, 74.5, makes another trip to Rome, during which he visits Pope Benedict XV, having been commissioned to execute a portrait bust of the new pope.

July – His sculptures The Burghers of Calais, purchased by England in 1912, are quietly unveiled in Victoria Gardens, outside the Houses of Parliament in London.

Exhibition at the Royal Scottish Academy, Edinburgh, of sixteen of the eighteen sculptures, that Rodin donated to England, opened.

1916 – Rodin, 75.6, commenced his final work (which remained unfinished), the Bust of Etienne Clémentel (bronze, Musée Rodin, Paris), then Minister of Trade, Industry, Post and Telegraph, to thank him for the decisive role he played in restarting negotiations for the founding of a Rodin museum.

Rodin was seriously ill, because of a stroke which left him in a state of mental lethargy; with the damage being irreversible.

He offers to donate all his works to the French nation in three stages (1 April, 13 September, 25 October), on condition that the Hôtel Biron is converted into a museum in his honor. The Chambre des Députés, then the Sénat, accepted the donation, and the Assemblée Nationale voted in the establishment of the Musée Rodin in the Hôtel Biron.

Holland commissioned him a monument to commemorate the defense of Verdun.

1917 – 29 January - Rodin, 76.2, married Rose Beuret, 72.6, in Meudon.

14 February - Rose Beuret, now Rodin's wife for 16 days, passed away at 72.7, (1844 – 1917), in Meudon.

17 November - François Auguste René Rodin passed away at 77 years and 5 days, in Meudon.

24 November – Rodin was buried beside Rose in Meudon. A large-scale cast of his sculpture The Thinker was erected on their grave.

1919 – 4 August - The Musée Rodin opens to the public on 4 August, and holds over 6,000 sculptures, 7,000 of his drawings and prints, in chalk and charcoal, and thirteen drypoints. He also produced a single lithograph. The Musée Rodin is in the former Hôtel Biron (1727 – 1732, 77 Rue de Varenne, 240 m east of Tombeau de Napoléon Ier in Les Invalides).

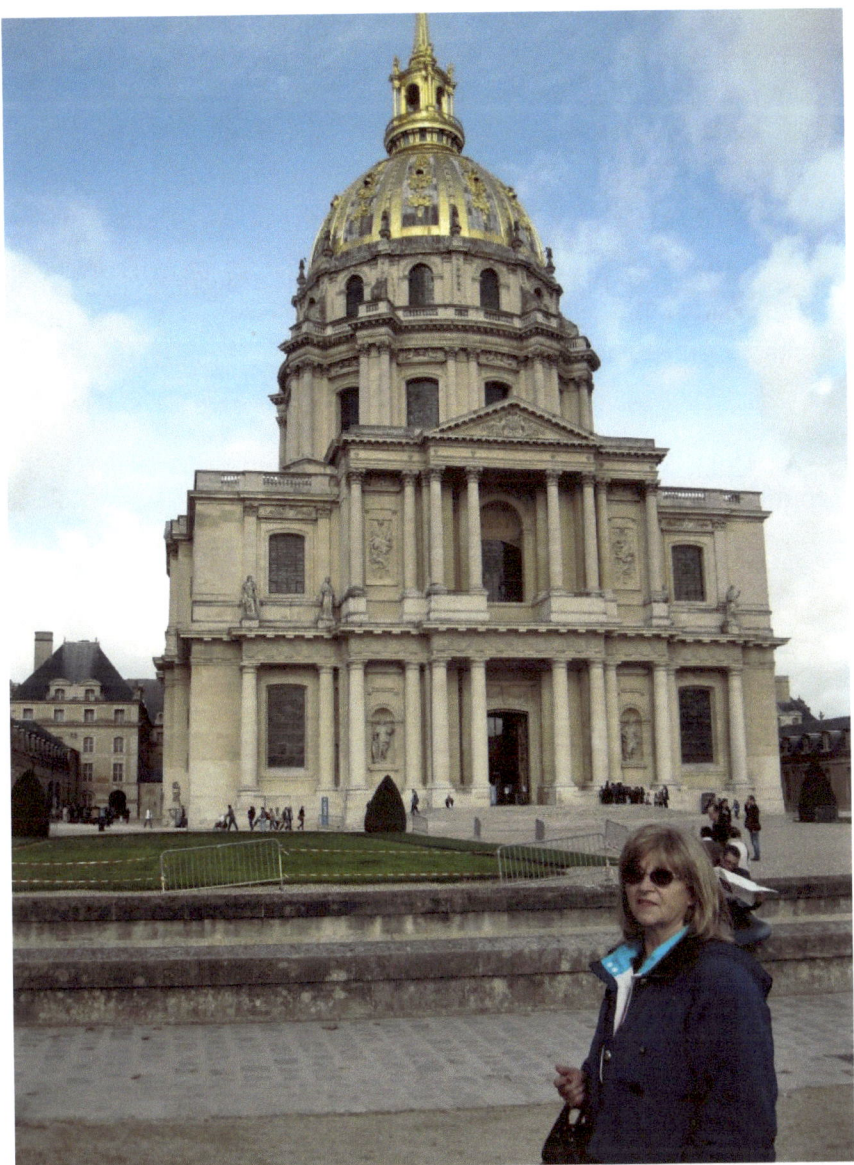

Église du Dôme (1708, 107 m height, inspired by St. Peter's Basilica in Rome,1626) in the center of L'Hôtel National des Invalides (1678, by Louis XIV, in the 7th arrondissement, with military museums and monuments and the burial site for Napoleon Bonaparte (1769-1821)). Napoleon was entombed under the Dôme of the Invalides, in a tomb made of red quartzite and resting on a green granite base, which was finished in 1861.

1926 – 5 December – 9 years and 18 days after Auguste Rodin passed away, the two days younger Claude Monet passed away, aged 86 years and 3 weeks (14 Nov 1840 – 5 Dec 1926, French painter).

1957 – 16 March – the former student of Rodin, Constantin Brâncuși, passed away aged 81 years and 25 days (19 Feb 1876, Hobița, Gorj, Romania – 16 March 1957, Paris, France, Romanian sculptor, painter and photographer, who made his career in France).

1963 – 8 January - Leonardo da Vinci's (1452 in Vinci, Republic of Florence, now Italy – 1519 in Amboise, Kingdom of France) *Mona Lisa* (or la Gioconda, 1503 – 1507, Louvre, Paris, France) is exhibited in the United States for the first time, at the National Gallery of Art in Washington, D.C.

2001 – Leonardo's vision of a bridge for the Golden Horn was resurrected in this year, when a smaller bridge based on his design was constructed in Norway.

2007 – 7 December - a red chalk sketch for the dome of St Peter's Basilica, possibly the last made by Michelangelo before his death, was discovered in the Vatican archives. It is extremely rare, since he destroyed his designs later in life. The sketch is a partial plan for one of the radial columns of the cupola drum of Saint Peter's.

2011 – Davinciite, a recently described mineral recognized in 2011 by the International Mineralogical Association, is named in honor of Leonardo.

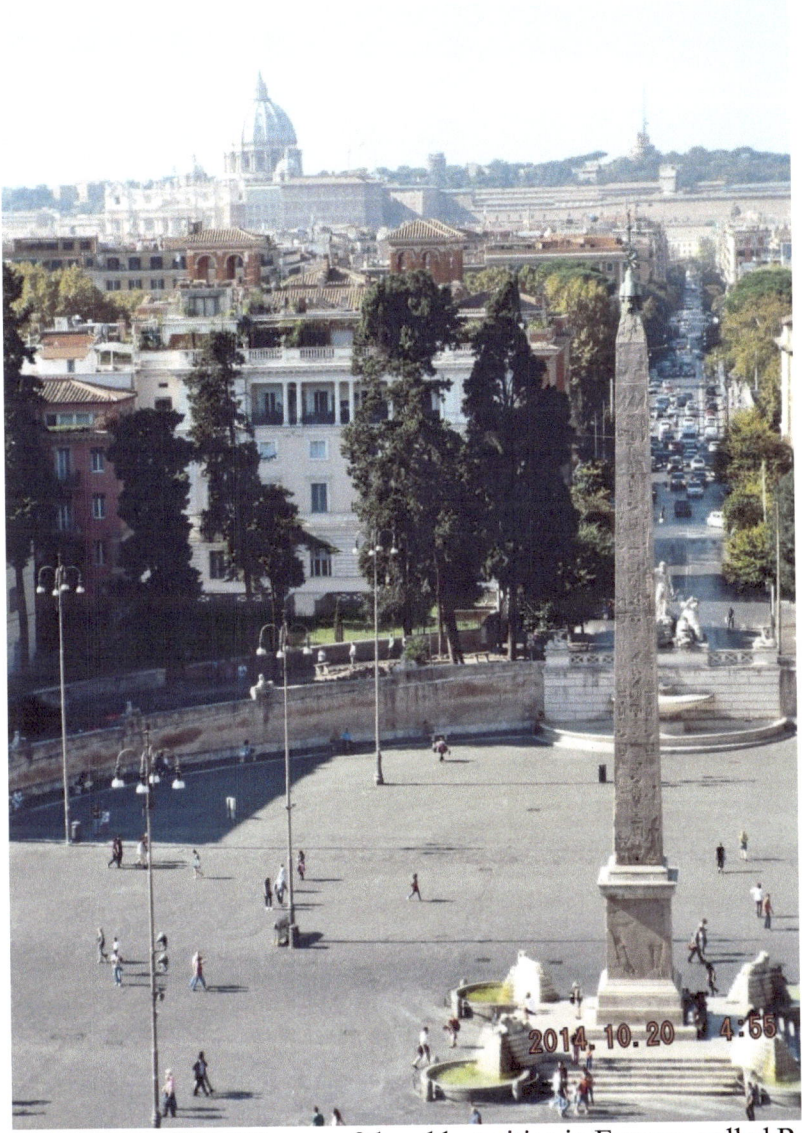

Italy, Rome (753 BC, one of the oldest cities in Europe, called Roma Aeterna (The Eternal City) and Caput Mundi (Capital of the World)), from the Pincian Hill looking southwest: Piazza del Popolo (1822), with the Egyptian obelisk (36 m) of Sety I (1290–1279 BC) and Rameses II (1303, 1279–1213 BC) from Heliopolis, brought in 10 BC by Augustus (63 BC-14 AD) for Circus Maximus, in 1589 here. Basilica San Pietro (1506, 132 m, back).

Bibliography

"The Histories" by Polybius
"Discours de la Méthode" by René Descartes
"Meditationes de prima philosophia" by René Descartes
"Philosophiae Naturalis Principia Mathematica" by Isaac Newton
Chinese encyclopedia Gujin Tushu Jicheng (Imperial Enciclopaedia)
"Encyclopédie" by Jean-Baptiste le Rond d'Alembert and Denis Diderot
"Encyclopaedia Britannica" by over 4,400 contributors
"Encyclopedia Americana" by Francis Lieber
"Grand Larousse encyclopédique en 24 volumes" by Albert Ducrocq
"Great Russian Encyclopedia" by Yury Osipov
"Encyclopedia of China"
"Enciclopedia Italiana di Scienze, Lettere ed Arti" (35 volume), by Giovanni Treccani
"Allgemeine Encyclopädie der Wissenschaften und Künste" by Johann Samuel Ersch und Johann Gottfried Gruber
"Gran Enciclopedia de España"

Michael M. Dediu is also the author of these books (which can be found on Amazon.com):

1. Aphorisms and quotations – with examples and explanations
2. Axioms, aphorisms and quotations – with examples and explanations
3. 100 Great Personalities and their Quotations
4. Professor Petre P. Teodorescu – A Great Mathematician and Engineer
5. Professor Ioan Goia – A Dedicated Engineering Professor
6. Venice (Venezia) – a new perspective. A short presentation with photographs
7. La Serenissima (Venice) - a new photographic perspective. A short presentation with many photos

8. Grand Canal – Venice. A new photographic viewpoint. A short presentation with many photos
9. Piazza San Marco – Venice. A different photographic view. A short presentation with many photos
10. Roma (Rome) - La Città Eterna. A new photographic view. A short presentation with many photos
11. Why is Rome so Fascinating? A short presentation with many photos
12. Rome, Boston and Helsinki. A short photographic presentation
13. Rome and Tokyo – two captivating cities. A short photographic presentation
14. Beautiful Places on Earth – A new photographic presentation
15. From Niagara Falls to Mount Fuji via Rome - A novel photographic presentation
16. From the USA and Canada to Italy and Japan - A fresh photographic presentation
17. Paris – Why So Many Call This City Mon Amour - A lovely photographic presentation
18. The City of Light – Paris (La Ville-Lumière) - A kaleidoscopic photographic presentation
19. Paris (Lutetia Parisiorum) – the romance capital of the world - A kaleidoscopic photographic view
20. Paris and Tokyo – a joyful photographic presentation. With a preamble about the Universe
21. From USA to Japan via Canada – A cheerful photographic documentary
22. 200 Wonderful Places, In The Last 50 Years – A personal photographic documentary
23. Must see places in USA and Japan - A kaleidoscopic photographic documentary
24. Grandeurs of the World - A kaleidoscopic photographic documentary
25. Corneliu Leu – writer on the same wavelength as Mark Twain. An American viewpoint
26. From Berkeley to Pompeii via Rome – A kaleidoscopic photographic documentary
27. From America to Europe via Japan - A kaleidoscopic photographic documentary
28. Discover America and Japan - A photographic documentary

29. J. R. Lucas – philosopher on a creative parallel with Plato, An American viewpoint
30. From America to Switzerland via France - A photographic documentary
31. From Bretton Woods to New York via Cape Cod - A photographic documentary
32. Splendid Places on the Atlantic Coast of the U. S. A. - A photographic documentary
33. Fourteen nice Cities on three Continents - A photographic documentary
34. 17 Picturesque Cities on the World Map - A photographic documentary
35. Unforgettable Places from Four Continents including Trump buildings - A photographic documentary
36. Dediu Newsletter, Volume 1, Number 1, 6 December 2016 – Monthly news, review, comments and suggestions for a better and wiser world
37. Dediu Newsletter, Volume 1, Number 2, 6 January 2017 (available at www.derc.com).
38. Dediu Newsletter, Volume 1, Number 3, 6 February 2017 (available at www.derc.com).
39. London and Greenwich, A photographic documentary
40. Dediu Newsletter, Volume 1, Number 4, 6 March 2017 (available also at www.derc.com).
41. Dediu Newsletter, Volume 1, Number 5, 6 April 2017 (available also at www.derc.com).
42. Dediu Newsletter, Volume 1, Number 6, 6 May 2017 (available also at www.derc.com).
43. Dediu Newsletter, Volume 1, Number 7, 6 June 2017 (available also at www.derc.com).
44. London, Oxford and Cambridge, A photographic documentary
45. Dediu Newsletter, Volume 1, Number 8, 6 July 2017 (available also at www.derc.com).
46. Dediu Newsletter, Volume 1, Number 9, 6 August 2017 (available also at www.derc.com).
47. Dediu Newsletter, Volume 1, Number 10, 6 September 2017 (available also at www.derc.com).

48. Three Great Professors: President Woodrow Wilson, Historian Germán Arciniegas, Mathematician Gheorghe Vrănceanu, A chronological and photographic documentary
49. Dediu Newsletter, Volume 1, Number 11, 6 October 2017 (available also at www.derc.com).
50 Dediu Newsletter, Volume 1, Number 12, 6 November 2017 (available also at www.derc.com).
51 Dediu Newsletter, Volume 2, Number 1 (13), 6 December 2017 (available also at www.derc.com).
52 Two Great Leaders: Augustus and George Washington, A chronological and photographic documentary
53. Dediu Newsletter, Volume 2, Number 2 (14), 6 January 2018 (available also at www.derc.com).
54. Newton, Benjamin Franklin, and Gauss, A chronological and photographic documentary
55. Dediu Newsletter, Volume 2, Number 3 (15), 6 February 2018 (available also at www.derc.com).
56. 2017: World Top Events, But Many Little Known, A chronological and photographic documentary
57. Dediu Newsletter, Volume 2, Number 4 (16), 6 March 2018 (available also at www.derc.com).
58. Vergilius, Horatius, Ovidius, and Shakespeare, A chronological and photographic documentary.
59. Dediu Newsletter, Volume 2, Number 5 (17), 6 April 2018 (available also at www.derc.com).
60. Dediu Newsletter, Volume 2, Number 6 (18), 6 May 2018 (available also at www.derc.com).
61. Vivaldi, Bach, Mozart, and Verdi, A chronological and photographic documentary
62. Dediu Newsletter, Volume 2, Number 7 (19), 6 June 2018 (available also at www.derc.com).
63. Dediu Newsletter, Volume 2, Number 8 (20), 6 July 2018 (available also at www.derc.com).
64. Dediu Newsletter, Volume 2, Number 9 (21), 6 August 2018 (available also at www.derc.com).
65. World History, a new perspective - A chronological and photographic documentary.
66. World Humor History with over 100 Jokes, a new perspective - A chronological and photographic documentary

67. Dediu Newsletter, Vol 2, N 10 (22), 6 September 2018
68. Dediu Newsletter, Vol 2, N 11 (23), 6 October 2018
69. Dediu Newsletter, Vol 2, N 12 (24), 6 November 2018

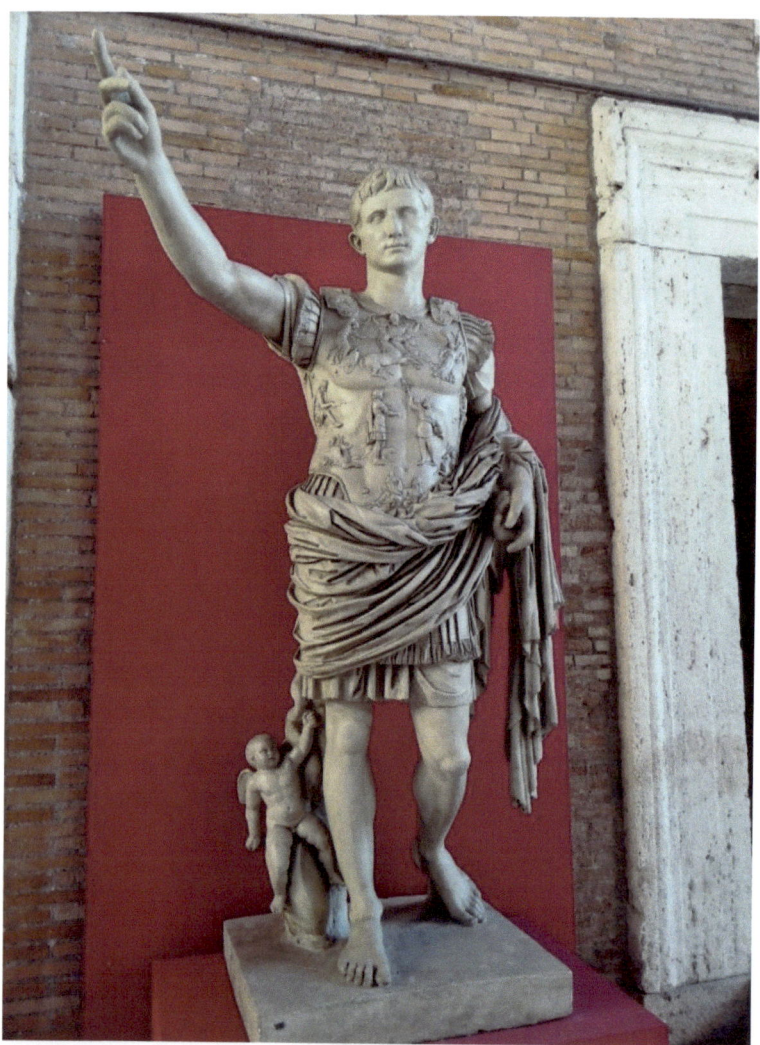

Italy, Rome (753 BC), a statue of Trajan (53 – 117), Roman Emperor from 98 to 117. The Roman Empire reached its greatest territorial extent under Trajan, through his conquests in the east (in Dacia, Arabia, Armenia, and Mesopotamia). Trajan's Market was an ancient mall that housed 150 shops and offices.

Michael M. Dediu is the editor of these books (also on Amazon.com):

1. Sophia Dediu: The life and its torrents – Ana. In Europe around 1920
2. Proceedings of the 4th International Conference "Advanced Composite Materials Engineering" COMAT 2012
3. Adolf Shvedchikov: I am an eternal child of spring – poems in English, Italian, French, German, Spanish and Russian
4. Adolf Shvedchikov: Life's Enigma – poems in English, Italian and Russian
5. Adolf Shvedchikov: Everyone wants to be HAPPY – poems in English, Spanish and Russian
6. Adolf Shvedchikov: My Life, My Love – poems in English, Italian and Russian
7. Adolf Shvedchikov: I am the gardener of love – poems in English and Russian
8. Adolf Shvedchikov: Amaretta di Saronno – poems in English and Russian
9. Adolf Shvedchikov: A Russian Rediscovers America
10. Adolf Shvedchikov: Parade of Life - poems in English and Russian
11. Adolf Shvedchikov: Overcoming Sorrow - poems in English and Russian
12. Sophia Dediu: Sophia meets Japan
13. Corneliu Leu: Roosevelt, Churchill, Stalin and Hitler: Their surprising role in Eastern Europe in 1944
14. Proceedings of the 5th International Conference "Computational Mechanics and Virtual Engineering" COMEC 2013
15. Georgeta Simion – Potanga: Beyond Imagination: A Thought-provoking novel inspired from mid-20th century events
16. Ana Dediu: The poetry of my life in Europe and The USA
17. Ana Dediu: The Four Graces
18. Proceedings of the 5th International Conference "Advanced Composite Materials Engineering" COMAT 2014
19. Sophia Dediu: Chocolate Cook Book: Is there such a thing as too much chocolate?

20. Sorin Vlase: Mechanical Identifiability in Automotive Engineering
21. Gabriel Dima: The Evolution of the Aerostructures – Concept and Technologies
22. Proceedings of the 6th International Conference "Computational Mechanics and Virtual Engineering" COMEC 2015
23. Sophia Dediu: Cook Book 1 A-B-C Common sense cooking
24. Sophia Dediu: Dim Sum Spring Festival
25. Ana Dediu and Sophia Dediu: Europe in 1985: A chronological and photographic documentary

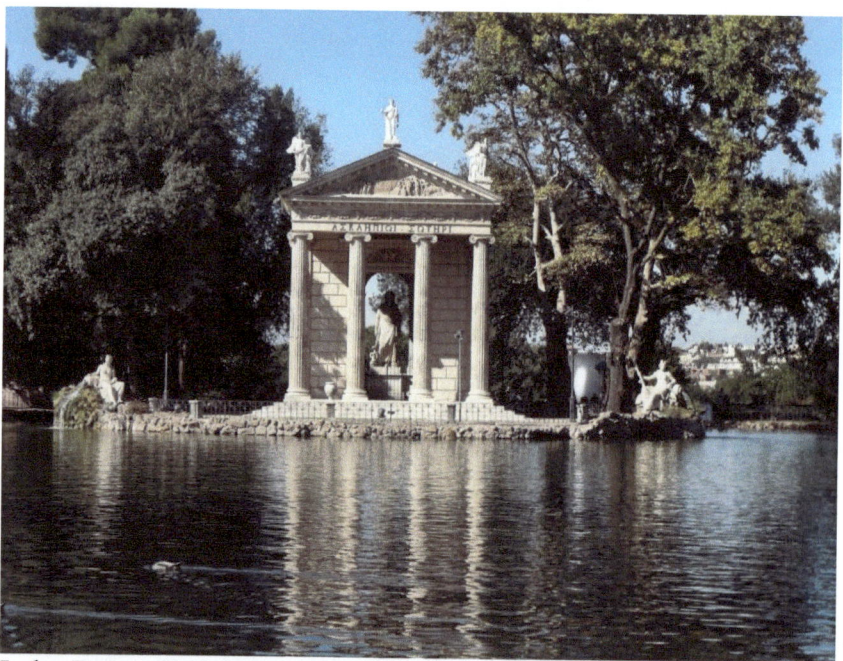

Italy, Rome (753 BC), Villa Borghese (1630), Lake Garden, from Viale del Lago, Tempio di Esculapio (1786, Temple of Asclepius (god of medicine, healing, rejuvenation and physicians)) on artificial island; on front, in Greek "To Asclepius the savior".

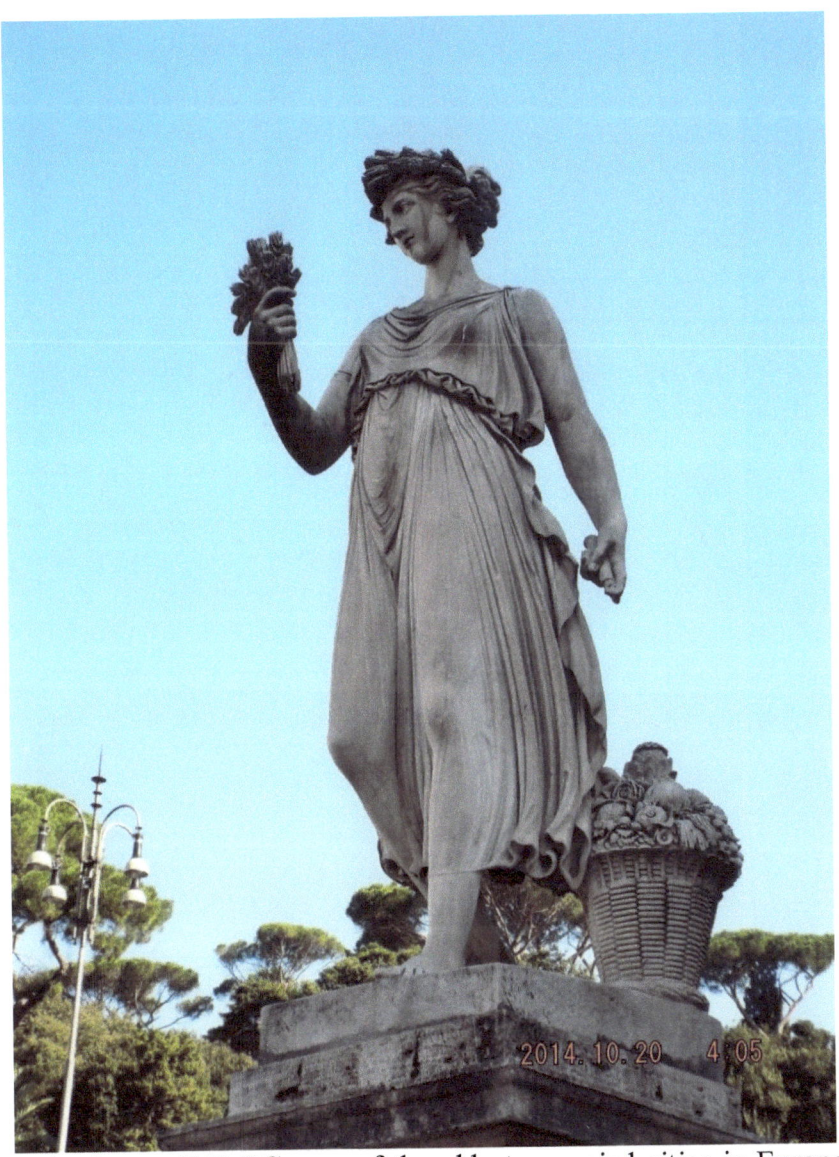

Italy, Roma (753 BC, one of the oldest occupied cities in Europe, called Roma Aeterna (The Eternal City) and Caput Mundi (Capital of the World)), southeast of Piazza del Popolo (1822, by Giuseppe Valadier, inside the northern gate in the Aurelian Walls, the Porta Flaminia, now called the Porta del Popolo), near Via del Babuino (opened in 1525 as the Via Paolina) and the church Santa Maria in Montesanto (1679, begun by Rainaldi and completed by Bernini and Fontana), the statue of the Goddess of Abundance.

www.ingramcontent.com/pod-product-compliance
Lightning Source LLC
Chambersburg PA
CBHW041940240526
45473CB00033B/12